BRITAIN'S BEST
HISTORIC SITES

This revised edition published in 2011 by New Holland Publishers (UK) Ltd

First published in the UK in 2007 by New Holland Publishers (UK) Ltd
London • Cape Town • Sydney • Auckland
www.newhollandpublishers.com

Garfield House, 86–88 Edgware Road, London, W2 2EA, United Kingdom
80 McKenzie Street, Cape Town 8001, South Africa
Unit 1, 66 Gibbes Street, Chatswood, NSW 2067, Australia
218 Lake Road, Northcote, Auckland, New Zealand

10 9 8 7 6 5 4 3 2 1

A catalogue record for this book is available from the British Library.

ISBN 978 1 84773 984 1

Publisher: Aruna Vasudevan
Senior Editor: Charlotte Macey
Designer: Colin Hall
Cartographer: Bill Smuts
Production: Sarah Kulasek

Reproduction by PDQ Digital Media Solutions Ltd, United Kingdom
Printed and bound in Singapore by Tien Wah Press (PTE) Ltd

BRITAIN'S BEST
HISTORIC SITES

From Prehistory to the
Industrial Revolution

TOM QUINN

Photography by
ANDREW MIDGLEY

NEW HOLLAND

CONTENTS

INTRODUCTION

Britain is particularly rich in historical sites. Almost everywhere you look are the marks of past human life. Villages, towns and cities are often built on top of earlier settlements. Even relatively remote countryside, such as the uplands of Dartmoor, often bears the marks of thousands of years of human activity.

Waves of immigration throughout history have contributed to the ethnic mix of the British peoples. Among the conquerors and settlers of the past are the mysterious, prehistoric people who built monuments such as Stonehenge, the Celts, the Romans, the Anglo–Saxons, the Vikings and the Normans. Archaeologists have found – and are continuing to find – many traces of these peoples among the stone ruins of their castles, their religious monuments and the remains of wooden houses, cooking utensils, bones, and even clothes. Each discovery enables us to understand more about how these people lived on a day-to-day basis, what was important to them and the illnesses or diseases that may have contributed to their demise. In 2004 the first mass Roman grave containing the remains of more than 90 people was discovered in Gloucester.

Experts believe that the bodies were dumped there following a virulent outbreak of disease in the 2nd or 3rd century.

Sites from more recent times include not just the castles and manor houses of the monarchy and nobility but also the remains of the once-widespread Catholic monasteries destroyed in England and Scotland after the 16th-century Protestant reformations – as well as farm buildings, flour mills, and early factories.

Archaeologists also believe that they have identified the site of the Battle of Towton (1461), which may contain the remains of several hundred men, making it Britain's largest mass grave.

THE SECTIONS

This book contains 85 of the most interesting and significant historic locations in the British Isles (including Ireland). It is divided into five sections, each covering a different era or epoch of British history – from prehistoric times to the Industrial Revolution.

The first section, 'Prehistoric Period', covers sites from several archaeological ages. These include the Lower and Upper

Palaeolithic (Old Stone Age): pre-8000BC; the Mesolithic (Middle Stone Age): 8000–4000BC; the Neolithic (New Stone Age): 4000–2500BC; the Bronze Age: 2500–700BC; and the Iron Age: 700BC–AD43.

Subsequent sections cover the 'Roman Period', which features places built during the Roman occupation of Britain from AD43 to 410; the 'Early Medieval Period', a time of the Anglo–Saxons and Vikings, between 410 and 1066, and the 'Late Medieval Period', covering sites that had their heyday from the time of the Norman Conquest in 1066 to 1485, when the War of the Roses ended in England. The concluding section of the book, 'Tudor to Industrial Period', features locations that were built after Henry VII (r. 1485–1509) ascended the English throne and stretches to the Industrial Revolution, which began in the late 18th century.

THE ENTRIES

Each beautifully illustrated double-page entry features the site's location, construction date and special features at the top of the entry. A concise essay gives an accessible overview of the place under discussion, describing its history and detailing any legends and people – such as monarchs or nobility – associated with it. The different phases of construction at the site or its uses are also examined and the author gives key information on when the site was abandoned or destroyed or about how it managed to survive to the present day – and finally when it became a preserved monument.

Useful contact details are featured whenever possible, including the site address, telephone number, an information website and transport links. This makes *Britain's Best Historic Sites* not just an essential reference source but also a useful travel guide for history enthusiasts wishing to visit these fascinating sites.

ⓘ information key

Contact details

 Telephone number

 Website

Transport links

 Car route

 Underground station

 Overground station

 Bus or coach service

 Ferry or boat service

PREHISTORIC PERIOD

PRE-8000BC–AD43

That vast stretch of time we call the 'prehistoric era' was far more complex and organized than we may imagine. Intricate trading routes and specialized manufacturing processes of various kinds created a relatively sophisticated world whose physical remains can be seen right across Britain to this day – indeed some of Britain's most famous and intriguing archaeological sites belong to the long period before the arrival of the Romans in AD43.

From the mysterious stone circles of Avebury and Callanish and the monumental remains of Stonehenge to carved hilltop images and graves, prehistoric Britain is a place of endless fascination for enthusiasts.

PREHISTORIC LOCATIONS

(1) Lanyon Quoit

(2) Cheddar Gorge and Gough's Cave

(3) Maiden Castle

(4) Avebury Ring

(5) Silbury Hill

(6) Stonehenge

(7) Old Sarum

(8) Wayland's Smithy

(9) Uffington White Horse

(10) Flag Fen

(11) Cresswell Crags

(12) Malham Tarn

(13) Castlerigg Stone Circle

(14) Carreg Samson Burial Chamber

(15) Creetown Cairn

(16) Mousa Broch

(17) Glenelg Brochs

(18) Clava Bronze Age Burial

(19) Callanish

(20) Skara Brae

(21) The Hill of Tara

(22) Dun Aonghasa

(23) Newgrange

16

20

19

Inverness

18

Aberdeen

17

EDINBURGH

Glasgow

Londonderry

Donegal

NORTHERN
IRELAND

BELFAST

Newcastle upon tyne

15

13

12

York

23

Liverpool

Manchester

11

21

DUBLIN

22

Galway

IRELAND

Caernarfon

ENGLAND

10

Norwich

Limerick

Birmingham

Cambridge

Waterford

14

Killarney

WALES

Oxford

LONDON

8

9

CARDIFF

Bristol

Exeter

2

5

4

6

7

3

Southampton

Brighton

Dover

0 10 20 30 40 50 60 miles

0 10 20   40   60   80   100 km

LANYON QUOIT

SITE LOCATION: **NEAR MADRON, CORNWALL** See map p.9 **1**

CONSTRUCTION DATE: **c.2500BC**

SPECIAL FEATURES: **NEARBY CISTS AND AN ANCIENT LONGSTONE**

The Neolithic chambered tomb known as Lanyon Quoit, built *c.*2500BC, consists of a huge capstone that weighs more than 12.2 tonnes (13.5 tons). This capstone is supported by three monumental upright stones. It was probably the burial chamber of a long mound. The remains of the mound can still be seen and it may originally have been as long as 18 metres (60 feet) and would once have been covered with turf.

In 1815, during a ferocious storm, Lanyon Quoit collapsed, but the site was restored in 1824 using three of the original four stones – the fourth was considered too badly damaged to put back in place. However, the reconstruction placed the structure at right angles to its original position, and the quoit we see today is considerably lower than it would have been before the storm damage: 18th-century visitors described riding under the capstone on horseback, something that would be impossible now.

Lanyon Quoit lies close to a number of similar sites: to the south are the remains of several stone burial boxes (also known as cists), and to the north-west a longstone hints at the presence of another ancient site.

Another name for the quoit is Giant's Table, or Giant's Tomb. This title relates to the local legend that a giant's bones were once found in the tomb.

◀ *The Neolithic Lanyon Quoit was probably the burial chamber of a long mound – about 18 metres (60 feet) in length – and would once have been covered with turf.*

ⓘ information

Contact details

Lanyon Quoit
Madron
Cornwall

☎ +44 (0)870 333 1181

 Lanyon Quoit
www.britainexpress.com
/counties/cornwall/ancient
/lanyon-quoit.htm

Transport links

 At the side of the
Morvah–Madron road,
West Cornwall

CHEDDAR GORGE
AND GOUGH'S CAVE

SITE LOCATION: NEAR BRISTOL, SOMERSET See map p.9 (2)
CONSTRUCTION DATE: 500,000BC
SPECIAL FEATURES: ANCIENT FIELD PATTERNS AND EARTHWORKS

This part of the Mendip Hills in Somerset has been inhabited for thousands of years and the effects of human activity on the landscape are rich and diverse – hunting and gathering, quarrying, farming and forestry have all left their mark.

The earliest archaeological evidence in the area comes from the caves, which still bear signs of our most distant ancestors. Some 500,000 years ago, early humans used flint tools here, while outside in the dense woodland large animals like rhinoceros and elk, now long extinct in these islands, roamed the landscape. Evidence from the Upper Paleolithic (40,000–10,000BC) and Mesolithic (8000–4000BC) periods is rich in the Cheddar Gorge area, particularly from Wookey Hole and Cheddar Gorge itself.

The bones of that most famous archaeological discovery – Cheddar Man – were found in Gough's Cave. Cheddar Man is believed to have lived some 7,000 years ago, at a time when life was nasty, brutish and short. With herds of large and dangerous animals roaming the countryside, eternal vigilance would have been the price of staying alive. Archaeological evidence from Cheddar and other sites of very ancient settlement suggest that, contrary to romantic notions of ancient people living in harmony with nature, they were in fact extremely destructive and wasteful. Animal remains show that ancient humans often hunted by driving herds of wild animals over cliff edges. They could then have eaten only a tiny fraction of the meat before the rest was too putrid to be of any use.

Apart from the many caves that were inhabited from earliest times, a number of earthworks – at Dolebury, Burledge and Burrington – reveal other forms of ancient habitation; there are hill forts in the area, and the remains of a Roman settlement can be found at Charterhouse Townfield.

By the late 18th and early 19th centuries, the first signs of the Industrial Revolution appear as villages become small industrial centres. With prosperity came larger

 At their peak, the sides of the ravine at Cheddar Gorge are the highest inland cliffs in the country.

houses; but, like earlier habitations, these tended to be built along the spring line, where water was easiest to obtain.

The Neolithic period (4000–2500BC) produced numerous long barrows in the area – Priddy Long Barrows and Ashen Hill Barrows, for example – as well as henge monuments. Remarkably, more than 300 Bronze Age round barrows have also been identified. But the most impressive remains are probably the Mesolithic cave burials at Avelines Hole and Burrington Combe.

ⓘ information

Contact details

Cheddar Gorge
and Gough's Cave
Cheddar, Somerset

 +44 (0)1934 742343

 Cheddar Cave and Gorge
www.cheddarcaves.co.uk

Transport links

On the B3135 to Somerset

MAIDEN CASTLE

SITE LOCATION: NEAR DORCHESTER, DORSET   See map p.9 ③
CONSTRUCTION DATE: c.300BC
SPECIAL FEATURES: ROMAN TEMPLE FOUNDATIONS

Three kilometres (2 miles) south of Dorchester in the heart of English writer Thomas Hardy's Wessex lies the biggest hill fort in Britain – Maiden Castle (the name comes from the Celtic *mai dun*, meaning 'great hill'), which covers more than 19 hectares (47 acres).

Archaeologists have found flint and bone implements and tools that suggest that human activity on this hill dates back to at least 3,000BC. The first stage of development was the building of a bank barrow some 0.5 kilometres (600 yards) long and running east to west. About 1200BC the site was then completely abandoned for reasons which have yet to be explained, but by 300BC human activity had resumed and work on the present hill fort was

▼ *The construction of Maiden Castle's defensive banks and ditches was an enormous undertaking.*

 The foundation of the 4th-century Romano–Celtic temple can still be seen.

begun. The original fort was situated at the eastern end of the hill and then gradually extended to the west.

Maiden Castle is defended by three concentric ditches, each with its associated ramparts. The ramparts would originally have been further strengthened with timber palisades, entered through massive timber gates positioned at intervals. Entrances through the ramparts were offset, to make any attack easier to fight off, for if invaders got through one gate they would then be trapped between two rings until they could work round to the next entrance gate.

The Celtic Durotriges tribe held Maiden Castle until the Roman invasion of AD43, soon after which it was overrun by the Second Legion Augusta. The fiercest fighting seems to have taken place at the eastern entrance, where archaeologists discovered the remains of 38 Iron Age warriors killed during a battle. In nearby Dorchester Museum you can see the skeleton of one of Maiden Castle's defenders, still with a Roman bolt fired from a ballista in his spine.

The foundations of a Roman temple have been found at Maiden Castle but little is known about subsequent activity here. The Saxons may have lived in the castle, but it has been unused for at least 1,400 years.

ⓘ information

Contact details

Maiden Castle
Cheddar
Somerset
BS27 3QF

 West Dorset Tourism site
www.westdorset.com
/site/things-to-do
/maiden-castle-p133633

Transport links

🚗 3 km (2 miles) south of Dorchester. Nearest major road is the A354

 Dorchester, 3 km (2 miles)

AVEBURY RING

SITE LOCATION: NEAR MARLBOROUGH, WILTSHIRE   See map p.9 (4)
CONSTRUCTION DATE: c.2500BC
SPECIAL FEATURES: ANCIENT RECONSTRUCTED AVENUE

Avebury's stone circle is one of the most impressive and important in Britain. It dates from about 2500BC and consists of a bank some 410 metres (450 yards) in diameter. Originally this was accompanied by a 9-metre (30-feet) deep ditch.

There are actually three circles of stones. The inner circles were probably built first and the outer circle and ditch added perhaps a century later. The outer circle originally encompassed two avenues running from two of the circle's four gates, which were positioned roughly at its

north, south, east and west points. The avenue from the southern gate survives, and has been partially reconstructed and lined with stones to show what it might have looked like. It led, it seems, to nearby Overton Hill. The other now obsolete avenue led to Beckhampton Long Barrow, hinting at the links that seem to have existed between many of the ancient sites in this area.

Archaeological evidence suggests that Avebury Ring was used almost continually for more than 700 years after it was first built. However, much of what can be seen today may well be a reconstruction of the ring. Many of the stones were damaged and removed by farmers during the 18th century. In the 1930s British archaeologist and businessman Alexander Keiller re-erected many of the stones. The Alexander Keiller Museum, located in Avebury, is full of prehistoric objects.

◀ *The purpose of the Avebury Ring is unknown, but it almost certainly had religious and ritualistic significance.*

 The stones were damaged in the 18th century then re-erected in the 1930s.

(i) information

Contact details

Avebury Ring
Near Marlborough
Wiltshire
SN8 1RF

☎ +44 (0)1672 539250

 National Trust site
www.nationaltrust.org.uk
/main/w-avebury

Transport links

🚗 1.6 km (1 mile) north of
the Bath road (A4) on
the A4361 and B4003

🚆 Pewsey, 16 km (10 miles);
Swindon, 18 km (11 miles)

SILBURY HILL

SITE LOCATION: NEAR MARLBOROUGH, WILTSHIRE   See map p.9 **5**

CONSTRUCTION DATE: *c.*1000BC

SPECIAL FEATURES: CENTRAL TO A VAST, RITUAL LANDSCAPE

Silbury Hill is one of the strangest structures in the world. It is called a hill, but in fact it is entirely artificial – and we have no real idea why.

The effort involved in building it without modern tools must have been prodigious. Largely undamaged, despite the passage of more than 3,000 years since its construction, the 40-metre (130-feet) high conical mound stands in the middle of the Wiltshire Plain. It is estimated that the amount of soil and rubble that had to be moved to make it rivals that of the Great Pyramid at Giza – one estimate reckons that 500 men working continuously seven days a week for 15 years could only just have completed the work.

The evidence that has been uncovered indicates that the hill began as a 6 metre (20 feet) mound which was later capped with chalk rubble and then raised dramatically to its present height by excavating a 7.6-metre (25-feet) deep ditch all the way around the hill and adding the excavated material to the top of the mound.

Silbury covers a little over 2 hectares (5 acres) and visitors are not permitted to climb it, but the hill can be appreciated just as well from the ground. Perhaps what is most interesting about the hill is that we still do not understand its purpose or its role in the centre of this vast ritual landscape that encompasses barrows of several types, Neolithic enclosures and stone circles.

 The 40-metre (130-feet) high mound of Silbury Hill dominates the Wiltshire plain.

information

Contact details

Silbury Hill
Avebury
Wiltshire

 +44 (0)870 333 1181

 English Heritage site
www.english-heritage.org.uk
/daysout/properties
/silbury-hill

Transport links

🚗 1.6 km (1 mile) west of West Kennet on the A4

🚃 Pewsey, 14.5 km (9 miles); Swindon, 21 km (13 miles)

STONEHENGE

SITE LOCATION: NEAR SALISBURY, WILTSHIRE   See map p.9 (6)

CONSTRUCTION DATE: c.2000BC

SPECIAL FEATURES: UNIQUE LINTELS

Stonehenge – Britain's best-known ancient monument and now a World Heritage Site – is one of the most photographed prehistoric structures, its image seeming to symbolize the ancient world in a way that is unique.

Work on the Neolithic circle we know today probably began about 3100BC, but from archaeological evidence the site had been important to people for thousands of years prior to that. Despite the difficulties of moving and erecting such huge stones at this early date, the henge was completed

with lintels level to within half a centimetre and forms an almost perfectly symmetrical circle. The great 17th-century British architect Inigo Jones was so impressed when he saw it in 1655 that he assumed it must be Roman work. In the 18th century, the great architect of Bath John Wood is said to have based the Circus in the spa town on Stonehenge.

The huge blocks of stone from which the circle is made were shaped and secured with enormous skill: the vertical connections

▼ *Despite their enormous size and weight, the blocks at Stonehenge are cut precisely to fit each other.*

were created using precisely cut and shaped mortice and tenon joints, the horizontals using tongue and groove joints. How this was achieved using only mauls (rounded stone tools) is still a mystery, because the blocks are made from exceptionally hard stone.

The circle as we see it today was probably complete by 2000BC, having been remodelled on several occasions over the previous 1,000 years; smaller changes were then made until about 1600BC.

We still do not know precisely why Stonehenge was built, although there are many theories. It may have been a temple or had huge astrological significance. Certainly, it was a centrepiece of a vast landscape of monuments and graves that stretches right across this part of England.

ⓘ information

Contact details

Stonehenge
Wiltshire
SP4 7DE

☎ +44 (0)870 333 1181

 English Heritage site
www.english-heritage.org.uk
/daysout/properties
/stonehenge

 Stonehenge site
www.stonehenge.co.uk

Transport links

 3.2 km (2 miles) west of Amesbury, on the junction of the A303 and A344/360

 Salisbury, 15.3 km (9½ miles)

22

OLD SARUM

SITE LOCATION: NEAR SALISBURY, WILTSHIRE   See map p.9 ⑦
CONSTRUCTION DATE: FROM 2500BC
SPECIAL FEATURES: PANORAMIC VIEWS

This hill, on the outskirts of modern Salisbury, has been inhabited for at least 5,000 years. The earthworks are the remains of an Iron Age hill fort. But the Romans came too, and after them the Saxons and Normans, who completed their motte-and-bailey castle in 1069. People continued to live on the site until the mid-16th century.

Roughly oval in shape, the hill fort covers 11 hectares (27 acres), with a single entrance through the bank and ditch on the eastern side. The site was once known as *Sorviadum*, meaning 'the fortress by the gentle river', and when the Romans occupied it several of their roads converged here. During the Saxon and later periods,

▼ Old Sarum has a wealth of fascinating medieval remains.

▲ *The ancient earthworks are the remains of an Iron Age hill fort.*

a flourishing town grew up within the ramparts. The mound of the Norman castle can still be seen, along with the foundations of the original Norman cathedral, built in *c.*1092. This was later destroyed during a ferocious storm.

The reasons for the site's abandonment include the difficulty of transporting water and provisions to the various buildings. People found it much more convenient to live on lower ground, and by 1220 the decision to build a cathedral in New Sarum (modern Salisbury) accelerated the end of Old Sarum's occupation.

Although virtually abandoned, in the 19th century Old Sarum became a byword for bad politics as the most notorious of the 'rotten boroughs' – places that retained a parliamentary seat even when there was no longer anyone to represent them. Rotten boroughs could be bought and sold, and a succession of wealthy and corrupt individuals bought the land at Old Sarum. This practice ended with the Reform Act 1832.

(i) information

Contact details

Old Sarum
Castle Road
Wiltshire
SP1 3SD

 **English Heritage site**
www.english-heritage.org.uk
/daysout/properties
/old-sarum/

Transport links

 3.2 km (2 miles) north of Salisbury, off the A345

 Salisbury, 3.2 km (2 miles)

24

WAYLAND'S SMITHY

SITE LOCATION: NEAR SHRIVENHAM, OXFORDSHIRE   See map p.9 **8**
CONSTRUCTION DATE: c.3500BC
SPECIAL FEATURES: ATMOSPHERIC SETTING

This Neolithic burial chamber sits high up on the Ridgeway long-distance path, and though perhaps the site has been over-restored, it is still possible to get a glimpse on this remote hilltop of one small part of England as it was more than 3,000 years ago.

Archaeologists believe that two ditches were originally dug to create a mound here. A wooden building was then erected on the mound and at least 14 bodies were then placed in the building. By 3500BC, the building had gone and the mound had been enlarged more or less to its present size.

At one end of the mound a cross-shaped, stone-lined chamber was then created, at the entrance to which six standing stones were placed. Archaeologists believe that at least eight bodies were interred here, but any grave goods that may have accompanied them were stolen long ago – probably in Neolithic times. Two of the standing stones are also now missing. It is not known when the tomb acquired its current name – Wayland was the Saxon god of smithing – but legend has it that if you leave a coin and your horse at the mound in the evening you will return in the morning to find the horse shod and the coin gone.

The stonework of the tomb lining is of exceptionally high quality – a tribute to the skills of the builders and remarkable when one considers the age of the tomb.

The stonework of the tomb at Wayland's Smithy is of exceptionally high quality.

---

 information

Contact details

Wayland's Smithy
Compton Beauchamp
Oxfordshire
SN6 8

 English Heritage site
www.english-heritage.org.uk
/daysout/properties
/waylands-smithy

Transport links

 On the Ridgeway;
1.2 km (¾ mile) north-east
of the B4000 (Ashbury–
Lambourn road)

UFFINGTON WHITE HORSE

SITE LOCATION: NEAR SHRIVENHAM, OXFORDSHIRE   See map p.9 **9**

CONSTRUCTION DATE: 1200–800BC

SPECIAL FEATURES: UFFINGTON HILL FORT

Oxfordshire's famous chalk carving of a horse is deeply etched into a hillside and is visible from as far as 32 kilometres (20 miles) away. Some doubt has been thrown on the ancient origins of the horse, which would have had to be scoured regularly by generations of local people to have survived as well as it has. This would have had to happen at a time when a carved white horse may well have been seen as a relic of pagan practices and beliefs. It is indeed difficult to understand why the medieval church would have permitted this attention to be given to a pagan site.

The horse's artistic qualities, however, have never been in doubt – indeed, with its stylized design it can seem strikingly modern. The artist Paul Nash said: 'It is a piece of design … more a dragon than a horse.'

The original purpose of the horse is unknown; different theories suggest that it had a religious purpose, was an emblem of a tribe or celebrated a victory in battle. By the 18th century, the horse had become the site of an annual fair. Booths and stalls were set up each summer at Uffington Castle, and a cheese-rolling competition was held. The annual fair came to an end in the 1850s.

There are wonderful views from the White Horse, especially to the north to the hills that surround Oxford. The site is now looked after by the National Trust.

 Despite its presumed age, there is something highly stylized and vaguely modern about the Uffington horse.

ⓘ information

Contact details

Uffington White Horse
Near Woolstone
Oxfordshire

 +44 (0)844 800 1895

 National Trust site
www.nationaltrust.org.uk/
main/w-chl/w countryside_
environment/w-archaeology/
w-archaeology-places_to_
visit/w-archaeology-
uffington_white_horse.htm

Transport links

 South of the B4507,
11.3 km (7 miles) west
of Wantage

FLAG FEN

28

SITE LOCATION: NEAR PETERBOROUGH, CAMBRIDGESHIRE See map p.9 **(10)**

CONSTRUCTION DATE: c.3000BC

SPECIAL FEATURES: BRONZE AGE RECONSTRUCTED HOUSES

It is extremely unusual to find a major site with large amounts of prehistoric wooden technology intact; yet that is just what was discovered in the waterlogged soil at Flag Fen in Cambridgeshire in 1982.

A remarkable place, Flag Fen features a wooden platform, the size of a modern football pitch, built about 3000BC and composed of some 60,000 timber posts driven into the ground in the correct alignment; yet we have almost no idea why this work was carried out at what must have been a huge expense of time and labour.

Flag Fen should be much better known because it is a site where visitors can see archaeology in action. Here, day by day, researchers are discovering things about our ancient ancestors, in many cases causing long-held views to be revised as a result of their findings.

On display in the museum at Flag Fen is the oldest wooden wheel in England and other remarkable timber artefacts. Axe heads have also been found here along with daggers and thousands of other items made from gold, bronze and tin.

Archaeologists believe that the site was hugely important for a number of Bronze Age rituals, as most of the objects found in the water here were almost certainly deliberately left, probably by the relatives of the recently dead. Many items had been deliberately broken or taken apart before being placed in the water.

◀ *An ancient stone coffin at Flag Fen.*

 A reconstructed house at Flag Fen; its design is based on precise and accurate archaeological evidence.

The remains of boats have also been found, and many of the objects recovered were made on the European continent or from raw materials sourced in Wales or the West Country – remarkable testimony to the complex trade interactions that existed.

(i) information

Contact details

Flag Fen, The Droveway
Northey Road, Peterborough
Cambridgeshire, PE6 7QJ

☎ +44 (0)1733 313414

 **Flag Fen**
www.flagfen.com

Transport links

🚗 Junction 5 of the A1139
or via the B1040 from
Whittlesey or Thorney

CRESSWELL CRAGS

30

SITE LOCATION:	WORKSOP, NOTTINGHAMSHIRE
HABITATION DATE:	c.60,000BC
SPECIAL FEATURES:	MUSEUM AND VISITOR CENTRE

See map p.9 (11)

The limestone gorge known as Cresswell Crags is a labyrinth of caves and underground pathways that show clear evidence of having been inhabited before the last ice age, between 60,000 and 40,000 years ago. There is further evidence of human habitation after the ice had retreated, from about 12000BC.

Masses of stone tools and animal remains were discovered here during numerous archaeological expeditions, but the most exciting find was made in 2003 when archaeologists discovered cave paintings deep within the complex.

Evidence suggests that Cresswell Crags was one of the most northerly places reached by ancient humans, and the whole gorge is carefully preserved – with much of its archaeology intact – as part of the Cresswell Heritage Landscape Area (CHLA).

Numerous ancient tools have been found right across the site. Made from flint and quartzite, these date from before the last ice age and it seems certain that the caves were inhabited by our earliest direct ancestors – *Homo sapiens* – rather than our close relatives, the Neanderthals – *Homo neanderthalensis*.

Many of the flints seem to have been brought here from much further afield, which suggests some sort of trading system. Barbed harpoon points have also been found, along with bone needles and a hearth.

Very simple art, in the form of stone engravings and incisions, had been found at Cresswell long before the 2003 discovery – one of the most exciting finds was a bone engraved with a stylized horse. Over the years, 80 other carvings have been found, including those that depict animals such as birds, bison, deer and bears.

Today the caves still enjoy the marvellous names they have been given in more recent centuries, including Mother Grundy's Parlour, Dog Hole and Church Hole.

At the east end of the gorge, there is a fascinating and well-organized museum and visitor centre. The caves are open to the public and guided tours are available (see website for further information).

 Cresswell Crags provided numerous cave complexes for our ancestors, who left carvings and incisions depicting animals such as birds, bison, deer and bears in the rocks.

ⓘ information

Contact details

Creswell Crags Museum
and Heritage Centre
Crags Road, Welbeck, Worksop
Nottinghamshire, S80 3LH

☎ +44 (0)1909 720378

www Cresswell Crags

www.creswell-crags.org.uk

Transport links

🚗 Crags Road is off
the B6042

🚆 Creswell, 1.6 km (1 mile)

MALHAM TARN

SITE LOCATION: YORKSHIRE DALES, YORKSHIRE   See map p.9 **12**

CONSTRUCTION DATE: VARIOUS PERIODS

SPECIAL FEATURES: 60 SIGNIFICANT SITES IN THE AREA

Malham, about 19.3 kilometres (12 miles) north-east of Skipton, is a spectacularly beautiful place. Part of the Yorkshire Dales National Park, it also has a huge wealth of archaeological remains, many of which are completely hidden beneath the waters of the famous tarn.

Recent studies have revealed more than 60 archaeologically significant sites in the area, ranging from medieval quarries, trackways and field systems through dew ponds to Romano–British structures.

Malham Tarn – a lake in an upland limestone landscape – has been the focus of human activity in the area for thousands of years. In 1791, however, the construction of a dam raised the water level and drowned much of the evidence of those centuries of human activity. Recent archaeology has attempted to rediscover this lost world.

Hearths from the 18th century have been discovered, together with a 17th- or 18th-century drinking glass and a collapsed dry stone wall made from massive blocks of stone – some of them as much as 2 metres (6 feet) across. We don't yet know who cut these blocks, but the research continues.

◀ *The tarn is slowly revealing its archaeological secrets, including trackways and dry stone walls.*

ⓘ information

Contact details

Malham Tarn
Settle, North Yorkshire
BD24 9PT

 National Trust site
www.nationaltrust.org.uk/
main/w-malhamtarnmoor

Transport links

 Take the A65 from Skipton to Gargrave, then follow signs to Malham. From Settle, follow signs to Langcliffe or Malham.

 Service 210/843 from Skipton or service 580/210 from Settle; alight at Malham, about 3.2 km (2 miles) from Malham Tarn

 Settle, 11 km (7 miles)

34

CASTLERIGG STONE CIRCLE

SITE LOCATION: NEAR KESWICK, CUMBRIA   See map p.9 **(13)**

CONSTRUCTION DATE: *c.*3200BC

SPECIAL FEATURES: PANORAMA OF RUGGED HILLS

Stone circles are quite common in Britain, but few are as spectacularly situated as Castlerigg in Cumbria. Surrounded by the wild hills of the English Lakes, it is a haunting monument to a civilization about which we know very little.

Most likely constructed about 3200BC, the 38 remaining stones are not arranged in a true circle at all, but are deliberately flattened slightly on the north side. Why this should be is unknown, but it may well have had significance for the long-vanished society that erected the stones. Just inside the eastern end is a group of ten stones now known as 'The Cove', the purpose of which is also unknown. Two larger stones flank a wide space to the north of the circle, which may well have been some kind of an entranceway. To the south, another stone stands alone and just outside the circle – its purpose, once again, unknown.

Some archaeologists believe that there were originally as many as 41 stones in the circle; of those visible today, some are still standing – to a height of about 1.5 metres (5 feet) – while others lie where they have fallen at various times in the past 3,000 to 4,000 years. That only three seem to have been lost makes Castlerigg Stone Circle among the best preserved in Britain.

Castlerigg is one of Britain's best preserved stone circles, but research shows that it is not actually a true circle.

---

 information

Contact details

Castlerigg Stone Circle
Keswick
Cumbria
CA12 4XX

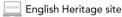 **English Heritage site**
www.english-heritage.org.uk
/daysout/properties
/castlerigg-stone-circle/

Transport links

   2.5 km (1½ miles) east of Keswick

   Service X4/5 from Penrith station to within 1.6 km (1 mile) of site

   Penrith, 26 km (16 miles)

CARREG SAMSON BURIAL CHAMBER

SITE LOCATION: NEAR FISHGUARD, WALES

See map p.9 (14)

CONSTRUCTION DATE: *c.*4000–2500BC

SPECIAL FEATURES: SPECTACULAR VIEWS

This Neolithic tomb, dating from some time between 4000 and 2500BC and also known as 'The Longhouse Cromlech' after a nearby farm, still has its massive capstone in place, supported by several huge upright stones. The capstone is over 1.8 metres (6 feet) above ground level and slopes down towards the bay and Strumble Head far beyond; this may have been part of the design built into it by its creators.

Earlier archaeologists believed that the tomb would originally have been covered with a mound of earth and stones, but opinions change, and the more recent view is that this kind of tomb may well have always been open to the elements in the same way as it is today, its contents intentionally left visible to onlookers for reasons at which we can only guess.

If the chamber at Carreg Samson was meant to be 'open' in the way it is now, the site may not have simply been a burial place in ancient times but had a more public and perhaps continual ritual significance. A location, in other words, where people may have gathered periodically.

 Wear and tear has changed the appearance of the tomb – several of the uprights no longer support the capstone, for example.

ⓘ information

Contact details

Carreg Samson Burial
Chamber
West of Abercastle
Pembrokeshire
SA62 5AN

 The Megalithic Portal site
www.megalithic.co.uk
/article.php?sid=1527

Transport links

 Close to Fishguard. It is located in a coastal sheep meadow, accessible over a cattle grid off the driveway of Longhouse Farm

38

CREETOWN CAIRN

SITE LOCATION: CREETOWN, SCOTLAND   See map p.9 **15**
CONSTRUCTION DATE: c.5000BC
SPECIAL FEATURES: PART OF A LARGE AREA OF ANCIENT SITES

Two well-preserved Neolithic burial chambers or cairns – usually described as Clyde-type burial chambers – can be seen near Creetown in this sometimes forgotten but very beautiful western corner of lowland Scotland. In fact, the whole of this area is littered with ancient burial sites, stone circles, Iron Age hill forts and other evidence of early human habitation, but Cairnholy I and Cairnholy II are particularly evocative.

These chambers were almost certainly part of a carefully planned, designed and integrated group of local burials. There is nothing haphazard about their positioning in the landscape, for they are oriented in

▼ *Despite the loss of much of the stonework these burial chambers remain impressive ancient monuments.*

a precise north–south alignment looking out across Wigtown Bay.

Situated close to a farm with the same name, the bigger of the two cairns, Cairnholy I, measures 43 metres by 10 metres (140 feet by 32 feet) and it reveals itself initially as a small stone chamber. Although the original capstone vanished long ago, the superbly cut and finished stone facade can still be seen. This gives us a clear glimpse into the ancient past, looking today much as it would have looked when the cairn was first built. Finds during excavation include Neolithic pottery shards, a hearth, an arrowhead and a fragment of a ceremonial axe.

Cairnholy II, on top of a small hillock, measures about 20 metres by 12 metres (65 feet by 40 feet). Legend has it that this is the tomb of the mythical Scottish king Galdus. This cairn is less well preserved and impressive than Cairnholy I.

 The skill of the tomb builders is revealed in the shape and positioning of the stones.

Much of what would once have been elaborate stonework surrounding both cairns has been stolen over the centuries, but the burial chambers are well worth a visit.

(i) information

Contact details

Creetown
Dumfries and Galloway
Scotland

Ancient Stones site

www.ancient-stones.co.uk
/dumfries/001/007/
details.htm

Transport links

 The site is signposted from the A75 between Gatehouse of Fleet and Newton Stewart. Take the narrow, single-track road

MOUSA BROCH

SITE LOCATION: SHETLAND, SCOTLAND   See map p.9 **16**

CONSTRUCTION DATE: c.200BC–AD200

SPECIAL FEATURES: WILDLIFE ON THE ISLAND

Among the great archaeological treasures of Scotland are the Iron Age brochs, those extraordinary circular stone towers, some 500 and more of which are scattered across the north and west of the country. The most impressive broch is found on the now uninhabited island of Mousa.

Scotland's brochs all seem to have been constructed between 200BC and AD200. Most are badly damaged, but Mousa – an extraordinary feat of ancient engineering –

▼ *Mousa Broch from above, revealing its wall structure.*

still stands more than 12 metres (42 feet) high. It was almost certainly built as one of a pair to guard the entrance to Mousa Sound. What remains of its twin broch can still be seen on the other side of the sound at Burrland.

The most immediately striking thing about the broch, apart from its great height, is the sheer thickness of its walls: it is 15 metres (50 feet) in diameter at its base, and at this point the walls are an incredible 4.5 metres (15 feet) thick. Within the massive thickness of the walls there are numerous chambers, which may have been used for storage or for some other purpose that we can now only guess at.

Once through the entrance, the visitor finds himself on a solidly built stone staircase that runs up and around the interior of the broch. Halfway to the top of the staircase is a landing, and there may well once have been a platform here that ran around the full circumference of the inside of the broch. Having passed the landing, one continues up the steps to the top of the broch, where there is a walkway

 Mousa Broch is the finest example of an Iron Age tower, of which there were roughly 120 in Shetland alone.

— the perfect spot from which to stare out over the sea and at approaching ships and potential enemies.

Despite its impressive bulk and superb architecture, almost nothing is known about the broch or those who built it; there is little else in the vicinity to suggest that it was part of a group of buildings, so it does not appear to have been the central part of a settlement of any kind. We are ineluctably led back to the idea of Mousa Broch as an isolated watch tower.

ⓘ information

Contact details

Mousa Broch
Island of Mousa
Shetland

 Undiscovered Scotland site

www.undiscoveredscotland.
co.uk/mousa/mousabroch/
index.html

Transport links

Accessible by boat from
Sandwick, about 22.5 km
(14 miles) south of Lerwick

GLENELG BROCHS

SITE LOCATION: NEAR GLENELG, SCOTLAND   See map p.9 (17)

CONSTRUCTION DATE: c.200BC–AD200

SPECIAL FEATURES: NEARBY 18TH-CENTURY BARRACKS

Near the village of Glenelg, on the shores of Glenelg Bay, are three remarkable brochs. They can be found just inland at Gleann Beag. The biggest and best preserved of the three is Dun Telve, its walls standing in places to a little over 10 metres (32 feet) high. Less well preserved but equally fascinating is the nearby Dun Troddan; its walls stand to about 7 metres (23 feet) in places.

Dun Troddan, and to a lesser extent Dun Telve, suffered during the building of nearby Bernera Barracks in the aftermath of the Jacobite Risings of 1715. Stone from the brochs was plundered by the barrack builders to save the cost and effort of carting stone from further afield. Completed in 1723, the barracks remain impressive and it is worth visiting the ruin today. Four such barracks were built across the Highlands to provide a garrison for the British sent to control the local population.

The third of the brochs in the Glenelg region is Dun Grugaig which stands 3.2 kilometres (2 miles) further east along Gleann Beag but little remains of it today.

Brochs generally seem to have been used for defence, but there is no hard evidence of this role and in the absence of such proof another theory suggests that they were actually the homes of the local aristocracy.

 Brochs are unique to Scotland but are regarded by archaeologists as part of a group of buildings known as Atlantic roundhouses.

ⓘ information

Contact details

Glenelg Brochs
Glenelg
Inverness
Scotland

 **Glenelg Broch site**
www.lochalsh.co.uk
/glenelg_broch.shtml

Transport links

 South of the village of Glenelg, the well-signposted brochs are situated in a field

44

CLAVA BRONZE AGE BURIAL

SITE LOCATION: NEAR INVERNESS, SCOTLAND   See map p.9 **18**

CONSTRUCTION DATE: c.2000BC

SPECIAL FEATURES: PART OF A WIDER ARCHAEOLOGICAL SITE

This remarkable site consists of three circles of standing stones, each enclosing a massive cairn. Each cairn has an inner chamber built from large stones and an outer stone kerb. The cairns have a distinct regional feel to them. Their shape and structure are typical of cairns found around Inverness and the Black Isle.

At the entrance to the site stands a substantial cairn some 32 metres (103 feet) in diameter, surrounded by a stone circle.

The cairn itself is entered via a passage that would originally have been covered, though it is now open – the result, no doubt, of stones being plundered from the site by local farmers as building material for homes and animal shelters. The burial chamber at the centre is also now uncovered.

The cairns are clearly linked to each other – their design is similar and the two entrance passages (the central cairn has no entrance passage) are aligned precisely

▼ *The burial chamber and passage would originally have been beneath a substantial mound of stones.*

 Each cairn is surrounded by a stone circle, the cultural significance of which is lost in the mists of time.

with each other along a line that also passes directly through two of the standing stones that surround the central non-aligned cairn. It is thought that the graves are Neolithic (*c.*4000–2500BC) and much earlier than the stone circles, which may have been erected during the Bronze Age (*c.*2500–700BC).

The cultural significance of this arrangement is not known, although the alignment of the passages points to the position in which the midwinter sun sets.

The site was almost certainly a burial place for the elite of the tribe that created the cairns rather than a general burial place.

 # information

Contact details

Clava Bronze Age Burial
Balnuaran of Clava
Near Inverness
Scotland

Undiscovered Scotland site
www.undiscoveredscotland
.co.uk/inverness/clavacairns
/index.html

Transport links

10 km (6 miles) east of Inverness. Signposted from the B9091, close to Culloden battlefield

CALLANISH

SITE LOCATION: ISLE OF LEWIS, SCOTLAND   See map p.9 **(19)**
CONSTRUCTION DATE: c.2000BC
SPECIAL FEATURES: THE STONES APPEAR TO MARK POINTS
                            IN THE LUNAR CYCLE

The Hebridean island of Lewis is home to one of the best groups of ancient standing stones in the country. The circle of 13 stones still stand to an impressive height of between 2.5 to 4 metres (8–13 feet). In the centre of the circle is a single, much taller stone rising to about 5 metres (16 feet). The centre of the circle also has the remains of an ancient tomb, but this was almost certainly added long after the first stones were erected.

The Callanish circle and more than 30 other stones combine to form a complex known as Calanais I. Northwards from the main circle of 13 stones heads an avenue formed from a double row of stones; the avenues that leave the circle in other directions are formed from only single lines of stones.

The main circle and the double avenue leading north have been dated to about 2000BC, while the avenues of single stones and the central tomb date from about 1500BC.

By 800BC at the latest, the site seems to have fallen into disuse and warmer, wetter weather rapidly increased the rate at which the surrounding peat bog grew, effectively covering much of the site. When it was cleared in the 19th century, an astonishing 2 metres (6 feet) of peat was found to have accumulated around and above the stones.

Not far from the main circle are further groups of stones. Calanais II consists of a circle of 10 stones 18 metres (60 feet) in diameter; but only five stones are still standing. A short distance to the south-east of Calanais I is Calanais III, consisting of 20 stones set out to create a double ring with a diameter of 16 metres (53 feet). Finally, on a nearby hill is Calanais IV – five stones set in an oval and surrounding a stone enclosed in a cairn.

Each of the Callanish monuments seems to have been carefully sited to ensure that each structure was visible to all the others. The explanation for the distribution and precise location of the stones currently considered most likely is that they marked various points in the lunar cycle. However, one local legend says that the stones are the remains of local giants who, having refused to become Christian, were turned to stone by the saints.

▲ *The circle of stones at Callanish includes a central stone, which stands far higher than those that surround it.*

(i) information

Contact details

Calanais Visitor Centre
Calanais, Isle of Lewis
Western Isles
Scotland
HS2 9DY

☎ +44 (0)1851 621422

[www] Calanais Visitor Centre site
www.callanishvisitorcentre.co.uk

Transport links

 From Stornoway, via Acamor and Gearraidh na h-aibhne on the A858, take the first left turn into Calanais and follow the road until you arrive at the visitor centre

SKARA BRAE

SITE LOCATION: ORKNEY, SCOTLAND   See map p.9 (20)

CONSTRUCTION DATE: c.3100BC

SPECIAL FEATURES: HUT INTERIORS

The existence of the Neolithic village of Scara Brae on Orkney's Bay of Skaill was unknown until one winter's night in the 1850s. A violent storm destroyed a section of the sand dunes and uncovered what was to become one of the most remarkable sites in Scotland.

The huts are remarkably preserved. The walls are made from sandstone slabs and each hut is linked to the others by passageways. In the surviving interiors, a flagstone dresser still stands, and there is a stone rectangular hearth in the centre of one of the huts. In the thick walls, what look like beds have been made from upright slabs, and above them are storage recesses and shelves.

Each of the huts also contains a stone box lined with clay, suggesting that they may well have been used for storing water.

Among the fascinating discoveries are the bones of whales, red deer and fish. Other finds such as intricately decorated pottery, as well as carefully crafted tools and weapons, suggest that this isolated community included highly skilled craftspeople who also knew enough to grow cereal crops.

Excavations have revealed that village life came to an end almost overnight. Some disaster may have befallen the inhabitants, who appear to have left so quickly that they did not even have time to gather their personal possessions.

 The complex village of Skara Brae lies in a picturesque part of the British Isles.

(i) information

Contact details

Skara Brae
Orkney
KW16 3LR

 Skara Brae site
www.historic-scotland.gov.uk
/index/places/propertyresults
/propertyoverview.htm?Propl
D=pl_244&

Transport links

 32 km (19 miles)
north-west of Kirkwall
on the B9056

THE HILL OF TARA

51

SITE LOCATION: COUNTY MEATH, IRELAND See map p.9 **21**

CONSTRUCTION DATE: c.2500BC

SPECIAL FEATURES: MYSTERIOUS CARVED ENTRANCE STONE

The Hill of Tara (*Temair in gaeilge*), was once the ancient seat of the High Kings of Ireland. In prehistoric and ancient times, 142 kings are said to have reigned there. It is also home to the so-called 'Mound of the Hostages', a megalithic tomb and the oldest monument on the hill.

The Mound of the Hostages was built some time between 3000 and 2500BC. It consists of a passage that is 4 metres (13 feet) long subdivided into three small areas. More than 200 separate cremations have been discovered there but the tomb's main interest today stems from the wonderfully engraved stone near the entrance. The patterns that adorn it have been variously interpreted as representing heavenly bodies – some kind of calendar – or as having some religious significance.

The distinctly phallic standing stone known in Irish as *Lia Fail* ('The Stone of Destiny') was moved to its current position on the hill in the early 19th century; before that it stood close to The Mound of the Hostages and may have been an entrance stone – a similar stone guards the entrance to the passage tombs at Knowth.

The Hill of Tara is rich in ancient sites: there are over 30 visible monuments, and perhaps many more buried beneath the earth.

 More than 200 separate cremations have been discovered at Tara's hill-top megalithic tomb.

ⓘ information

Contact details

The Hill of Tara
Navan, County Meath
Ireland

[www] Heritage Ireland site

www.heritageireland.ie
/en/midlandseastcoast
/hilloftara

Transport links

 12 km (7½ miles) south of Navan, off the N3

DUN AONGHASA

SITE LOCATION: ARAN ISLANDS, IRELAND
CONSTRUCTION DATE: c.1500BC
SPECIAL FEATURES: CLIFF-TOP LOCATION

See map p.9

One of the world's most spectacularly situated ancient monuments, the fort of Dun Aonghasa clings to the cliffs on the edge of Inishmore in the Aran Islands – one of the most remote spots in Europe.

Constructed during the Bronze Age, more than 3,500 years ago, it is battered by fierce gales that roar in across the Atlantic. Dun Aonghasa may well have been the Bronze Age equivalent of a royal or aristocratic palace where the ruling family or families of the local tribe lived. It is made up of a series of stone enclosures covering more than 5.5 hectares (14 acres) and encompassed by a final outer stone ring that would have been used to protect livestock. The middle and inner circles of stone protected the inhabitants of the fort: the innermost wall is a remarkable 5 metres (16 feet) thick. Originally it would have been as much as 6 metres (20 feet) high and taken more than 6,600 tonnes (6,500 tons) of stone to build.

Right at the edge of the high cliff, and in the centre of the inner enclosure, there was a rock platform, on which it is thought inhabitants of the fort performed ancient rituals. Archaeological evidence suggests that the fort was inhabited as long ago as 1500–1000BC, but activity here reached a peak in about 800BC.

High up on the precarious cliff top, Dun Aonghasa may have been a royal or aristocratic palace. ▶

ⓘ information

Contact details

Dun Aonghasa
Aran
County Galway

+353 (0)99 61008

 Heritage Ireland site
www.heritageireland.ie
/en /west/dunaonghasa

Transport links

 6.5 km (4 miles) west of Kilronan

 Tourist buses from Kilronan

NEWGRANGE

SITE LOCATION: KNOWTH, COUNTY MEATH, IRELAND See map p.9 **(23)**
CONSTRUCTION DATE: c.3200BC
SPECIAL FEATURES: STONES WITH MYSTERIOUS SPIRAL INCISIONS

Designated a World Heritage Site, the great tomb at Newgrange in Ireland's County Meath is a kidney-shaped mound covering a megalithic passage tomb. Archaeologists estimate that the tomb was constructed about 3200BC. The facade of white quartz is a restoration, but it hints at the former magnificence of this extraordinary site.

The mound above the tomb covers more than 0.4 hectares (1 acre) and is surrounded by kerbstones – 97 in all. Some of the stones are decorated with circles and whirls created long before the Celts arrived in Ireland (in the latter half of the first millennium BC). In other words, they are the art works of a mysterious, long-vanished people about whom we know very little.

Beneath the mound the tomb itself is magnificent, with a passage over 19 metres (62 feet) long leading to a cruciform chamber with a corbelled roof.

Like so many similar tombs and ancient monuments, Newgrange appears to have had some celestial significance; certainly the construction has been deliberately designed to allow a shaft of sunlight to penetrate the passage and light up the chamber on the winter solstice. This extraordinary event happens each year on every morning from 19 December to 23 December. At dawn on each of those five days, the sun pierces the tomb and the shaft of light remains shining down into the tomb for precisely 17 minutes.

▼ *The white facade of quartz is a restoration but it hints at the former magnificence of the site.*

So popular is Newgrange at this time of year that places to visit the tomb on these days are allocated by lot. The average number of applications is 27,000, from which 50 lucky names are chosen!

Evidence suggests that the mound may have originally been encircled by a series of standing stones; a dozen of these survive, but they are all at the front of the mound, giving rise to an alternative theory that they may have simply been part of an arc fronting at this part of the mound.

The most famous image from Newgrange is the tri-spiral – three concentric spiral incisions carved side by side and found on the stone known as 'Orthostat C10'. Described erroneously as Celtic, the spiral was carved about 2,500 years before the Celts, from whom the modern Irish are descended, reached the island. A similar large design appears on one of the entrance stones to the tomb.

Newgrange is remarkably similar to the 5,500-year-old Gavrinis tomb in Brittany; in this tomb the passage and chamber are lined with many carved stones, but it shares the underlying principle of construction with Newgrange.

(i) information

Contact details

Newgrange
Donore
County Meath

☎ +353 (0)41 988 0300

 Heritage Ireland site
www.heritageireland.ie
/en/midlandseastcoast
/brunaboinnevisitorcentre
newgrangeandknowth

Transport links

🚗 6.5 km (4 miles) west of Donore, south of the River Boyne

🚌 There is a bus service between Newgrange and Drogheda

ROMAN PERIOD

AD43–410

Enough physical evidence of Roman Britain survives to enable us
to see deep into the complex sophisticated society that the Romans
created. Because the Romans allowed the Celtic tribes of Britain to
continue their beliefs and religious practices, Romano–Celtic culture
became, to some extent, distinct from Roman culture. Villas were built
in the Mediterranean style for Celtic chieftains, as well as Romans, and
the remains of these splendid buildings are among the most exciting
archaeological sites in Britain today. Away from villas, forts and shrines
there are other famous Roman sites – Hadrian's Wall in the north
of England, and Bath, now designated a World Heritage Site.

ROMAN LOCATIONS

1. Bath
2. Tintagel
3. Portchester Roman Fort
4. Silchester
5. Pevensey Castle
6. Bignor Roman Villa
7. Fishbourne Roman Palace

8. Lullingstone Roman Villa
9. Welwyn Bath House
10. Chedworth Roman Villa
11. Letocetum
12. Wroxeter
13. Chester Roman Amphitheatre
14. York

15. Hadrian's Wall
16. Blackstone Edge Roman Road
17. Ribchester Roman Fort
18. Hardknott Roman Fort
19. Ravenglass
20. Dolaucothi Gold Mine

Shetland Islands

Inverness

Aberdeen

EDINBURGH

Glasgow

Londonderry

Donegal   NORTHERN   BELFAST
            IRELAND

Galway

DUBLIN

I R E L A N D

Limerick

Waterford

Killarney

15 Newcastle upon tyne

19

18

14 York

17

16 Manchester

Liverpool

13

Caernarfon

E N G L A N D

Norwich

12 11

Birmingham

Cambridge

W A L E S

20

10 Oxford   9

CARDIFF   Bristol   LONDON 8

1   4

Southampton   6 Brighton

3   5   Dover

7

Exeter

2

BATH

SITE LOCATION: BATH, SOMERSET   See map p.57 (1)

CONSTRUCTION DATE: 1ST CENTURY AD

SPECIAL FEATURES: ROMAN SCULPTURE AND VARIOUS ARTIFACTS

Bath was founded by the Romans in AD43 after they discovered the incredible natural spa. For a nation addicted to bathing, finding large amounts of spring water reaching the surface at a steady temperature of 48° Celsius (118° Fahrenheit) must have seemed quite literally a godsend to the Romans. They built a reservoir, baths and temples, and gradually a thriving sophisticated town grew up that was eventually to become the city we see today.

Bath – or *Aquae Sulis* as the Romans called their new town – has one of the best preserved Roman baths in Europe. Moreover, the size and sophistication of the baths reflect the social importance of bathing to the Romans. Here the Roman posted to Britain could enjoy a swim and take some exercise (in the *palaestra*) before having a warm bath (in the *tepidarium*), a hot bath (in the *caldarium*) or a cold dip (in the *frigidarium*). Then they could socialize and discuss the affairs of the day.

◀ *The bath spa complex is a wonderful mix of Roman and 18th-century architecture.*

Most of the Roman bath area in the modern town is still buried beneath later developments, but enough can be seen to give a clear idea of the size and scope of the complex which developed continually until the 4th century, just before the Romans abandoned Britain.

A vast hypocaust system heated a series of increasingly hot sweat rooms. There were also numerous swimming pools, cold rooms and five hot baths. At the centre of the whole complex and in its own elaborate hall was the great bath: this was lined with 14 huge sheets of lead and was surrounded by statues of the gods. It is the centrepiece of the baths as we see them today, although only the lower courses of the superstructure are Roman. The rest is largely 18th-century Georgian.

The temple of Minerva was located at the spring. Here an altar was built for animal sacrifice, and pilgrims who came to Bath from across the Roman Empire would throw coins and other offerings to the goddess. More than 20,000 coins have been recovered over the years, along with masses of written vows, curses and dedications that were scratched on pieces of lead and thrown into the waters – some are written backwards, which was thought to increase their magical strength. Curses usually asked that the person named on the scrap of metal should be punished for some alleged misdeed.

After the Romans pulled out of Britain, the buildings began to crumble and fall into ruin; rising water levels then began to damage the various structures, which would have collapsed fairly quickly. The Saxons used a great deal of stone from the Roman buildings for their churches. Eventually the site became marshy and for a time it even became a burial ground.

In the 18th century, an interest in the healing properties of mineral water arose again and Bath became a fashionable centre once more. The city was largely rebuilt, and taking the waters became a popular leisure activity. Today, visitors can see the baths but are not permitted to enter the water.

ⓘ information

Contact details

The Roman Baths
Stall Street
Bath, BA1 1LZ

 +44 (0)1225 477785

 The Roman Baths site
www.romanbaths.co.uk

Transport links

 Bath Spa

TINTAGEL

60

SITE LOCATION: NEAR WADEBRIDGE, CORNWALL   See map p.57 (2)

CONSTRUCTION DATE: C.AD1300

SPECIAL FEATURES: RUINED 13TH-CENTURY CASTLE

Despite its fame as the possible birthplace of the legendary British King Arthur of the late 5th and early 6th centuries, Tintagel has been neglected in recent years by all except hard-line Arthurians. This is a huge pity because Tintagel, situated in north Cornwall, Southwest England, has some of the world's most beautiful coastline, with unrivalled views out across the Atlantic.

The ruins of the castle at Tintagel date only from the 13th century, long after a wounded King Arthur is supposed to have

▼ *Tintagel is situated on the edge of the ruggedly beautiful Cornish coastline.*

departed for the island of Avalon, never to return, but they are still magical, especially when the autumn mists come in off the sea.

Just under a kilometre (½ mile) from the ruined castle is Tintagel Island and the ruins of what was once thought to be a monastery. It is now believed to have been a trading centre of a complex commercial network linking Cornwall with the Mediterranean.

Archaeologists have found masses of pottery fragments that have been traced to manufacturing centres in Spain, but little has been found, however, to confirm any of the Arthurian tales.

In the 19th century, Alfred, Lord Tennyson fuelled the Victorian interest in Arthurian legend with his cycle of poems 'Idylls of the King' (1856–85), which describes Merlin on Tintagel Island.

Ghostly presences have been described by visitors walking across the cliff tops in the late evening. It is certainly easy to imagine Arthur's Knights of the Round Table striding across this remarkable part of Cornwall.

 The ruins of the castle at Tintagel date back to the 13th century, but the site had been inhabited since prehistoric times.

ⓘ information

Contact details

Tintagel Castle
Cornwall
PL34 0HE

☎ +44 (0)1840 770328

 English Heritage site
www.english-heritage.org.uk
/daysout/properties
/tintagel-castle/

Transport links

🚗 On Tintagel Head, 600 metres (650 yards) along an uneven track from Tintagel village

🚌 Service 594/5 from Bude; service 584/594 from Wadebridge

PORTCHESTER ROMAN FORT

SITE LOCATION: NEAR PORTSMOUTH, HAMPSHIRE   See map p.57 **3**
CONSTRUCTION DATE: c.AD285
SPECIAL FEATURES: ROMAN FORTRESS

The Roman fort of Portchester, with its splendid views out over the Solent, boasts a wonderful mix of archaeological remains. In addition to having the most complete Roman walls in northern Europe, the fort also has a Norman keep and church, and the magnificent remnants of the palace of the Plantagenet king Richard II (r. 1377–99).

The fort covers 3.6 hectares (9 acres). Its walls are 6 metres (20 feet) high and 3 metres (10 feet) thick and made from flint interspersed with tiles and limestone. Along the seaward front there are D-shaped bastions at intervals: these were designed to be fitted with Roman catapults (ballista).

Portchester was originally part of a series of coastal defences built by the Romans, but it was also the scene of a remarkable act of rebellion by Carausias, a Belgian who was given the task by the Romans of clearing the English Channel of Saxon pirates in the late 3rd century AD. Carausias was so successful in this task, and became so rich from the booty he captured, that in AD285 he took over Portchester and declared himself Emperor of Britain. Carausias was eventually murdered, probably in 293 by Alectus, one of his assistants.

After the Romans left Britain, the Saxons appear to have held the castle until the Norman invasion of 1066. At the beginning of the 12th century, during the time of Henry I (r. 1100–35), a massive keep was constructed – it is still in remarkably good condition – and in the latter half of the 14th century, Richard II (r. 1177–99) constructed a great hall and added other domestic buildings. In fact, by this time Portchester Fort was to all intents and purposes a working royal palace.

By the mid-15th century the castle had declined – probably as nearby Portsmouth grew in importance – but it was used during the English Civil War (1642–51) to house troops, and again during the Napoleonic Wars (c.1803–15), when it served as a prison.

▲ *The massive Norman keep and Roman walls adjoin in this corner of the fort.*

ⓘ information

Contact details

Portchester Roman Fort
Church Road
Portchester
Hampshire
PO16 9QW

 English Heritage site

www.english-heritage.org.uk
/daysout/properties
/portchester-castle

Transport links

 South side of Portchester
off the A27; junction 11
on the M27

 Portchester, 1.6 km (1 mile)

SILCHESTER

SITE LOCATION: NEAR BASINGSTOKE, HAMPSHIRE   See map p.57 **(4)**
CONSTRUCTION DATE: C.AD85–300
SPECIAL FEATURES: COMPLETE ROMAN WALLS

Silchester, known to the Romans as *Calleva Atrebatum* (meaning 'the place in the woods of the Atrebates'), replaced and greatly extended a much older settled community established by the Celtic Atrebates tribe.

Today, few traces of the buildings that once stood here remain, with the exception of the town walls and the amphitheatre. The amphitheatre dates to AD85, making it one of the earliest completed in Britain.

Silchester is unusual in that it was simply abandoned after the Romans left Britain, but this has made it an archaeologist's dream. At first it was a timber settlement, but the main civic buildings had been rebuilt in stone by the end of the 2nd century, and by the 3rd century the town's walls had also been built in stone to an impressive height of nearly 6 metres (20 feet).

The town covered more than 40 hectares (100 acres) and within its standard Roman grid pattern of streets were a forum, three temples (one of which had 16 sides), baths and a basilica. Traces of about 180 stone houses have also been identified. Silchester burned down in the 3rd century, but like so many damaged or destroyed Roman towns it was quickly rebuilt.

◀ *Pasture now covers the remains of Silchester's houses and civic buildings. They lie within its still complete walls.*

(i) information

Contact details

Silchester
Church Lane
Hampshire

☎ +44 (0)1483 252 000

 English Heritage site
www.english-heritage.
org.uk/daysout/properties
/silchester-roman-city-
walls-and-amphitheatre

Transport links

 1.6 km (1 mile) east of Silchester

 Service 143 from Reading railway station to within 0.8 km (½ mile)

 Bramley or Mortimer, both 4.5 km (2¾ miles)

PEVENSEY CASTLE

SITE LOCATION: **PEVENSEY, EAST SUSSEX** See map p.57 **5**
CONSTRUCTION DATE: c.AD250–300
SPECIAL FEATURES: **NORMAN CASTLE WITHIN ROMAN WALLS**

Pevensey Castle is a remarkably complete Roman fortress in East Sussex. Built between AD250 and 300, it was designed to defend the south coast against invaders. The fort was constructed on what was then a small island known as Anderida, and its oval shape followed the lines of the island itself; this was unusual, as most Roman forts were rectangular in shape.

William the Conqueror (r. 1066–87) is said to have landed near Pevensey in 1066 and to have camped within the walls of the fortress. After the Saxons' defeat by William at nearby Battle, William gave the site to his half-brother Robert de Mortain. Robert built the castle within the Roman walls, some two-thirds of which can still be seen today. The Normans also established a mint in the fortress (rebuilt in 1342; its remains are opposite the main gate).

Pevensey was besieged by William II (r. 1087–1100), by King Stephen (r. 1135–41) and by Simon de Montfort in 1264. On several occasions the fortress was almost destroyed: Elizabeth I (r. 1558–1603) ordered it to be pulled down, but the order was not enforced. During Oliver Cromwell's rule (1653–58), the castle was sold to a builder, who planned to reuse its stones, but by 1660 it had been returned to the Crown.

 At Pevensey you can see the remains of the Norman royal mint, just opposite the main gate.

(i) information

Contact details
Pevensey Castle
Castle Road
Pevensey
East Sussex
BN24 5LE

 English Heritage site
www.english-heritage.org.uk
/daysout/properties
/pevensey-castle/

Transport links
 In Pevensey, off the A259
 Service 99 from Eastbourne
 Pevensey and Westham or Pevensey Bay, both 0.8 km (½ mile)

BIGNOR ROMAN VILLA

68

SITE LOCATION: PULBOROUGH, WEST SUSSEX   See map p.57

CONSTRUCTION DATE: AD190–300

SPECIAL FEATURES: MAGNIFICENT MOSAICS

This magnificent Roman villa boasts the longest stretch of continuous original Roman mosaic anywhere in Britain, some 73 metres (80 yards) in all, as well as other superb mosaics showing Minerva, Medusa, Ganymede, Venus and Cupid.

Bignor is situated in a beautiful position on the South Downs of West Sussex and houses a vast array of fascinating objects excavated from the site.

▼ *The bathhouse mosaic of Medusa.*

Villas in Britain were to some extent rural retreats for the Roman elite, but they were not just private houses. It is thought that many were also centres of rural activity, housing agricultural workers and other labourers as well as an elite family. Bignor may well fit into this category.

Villas built in the early period following the Roman invasion of AD43 tended to be constructed from timber; those built after the 2nd century AD were usually in stone, designed in the Mediterranean style with murals and mosaics and underfloor heating.

At the height of its prosperity, Bignor included as many as 70 buildings and covered 1.6 hectares (4 acres). The best-preserved parts of the villa are the rooms along the western end of the north wing and in the bathhouse section of the south-eastern corner. The finest surviving mosaics are here, including the long corridor mosaic which would originally have run the full length of the north wing.

Two dining rooms survive: one with underfloor heating was presumably the winter room; one without was more likely

 At the height of its prosperity, Bignor included 70 buildings and covered more than 1.6 hectares (4 acres).

to have been used in summer. Research suggests that this underfloor heating – the famous hypocaust system – was so effective that the inhabitants of a heated house would have had to wear sandals some of the time to avoid burning the soles of their feet.

The bathhouse here contains a fine mosaic decoration with the head of the Gorgon Medusa as the centrepiece.

The dining room has a mosaic that shows Venus and gladiators, while the so-called summer room has a mosaic of Ganymede carried by an eagle. A total of 11 rooms – impressive by any standards – retain their mosaics, and they are all open to the public.

It seems likely that, like so many similar sites, Bignor gradually fell into ruin after the Romans left Britain early in the 5th century.

(i) information

Contact details

Bignor Roman Villa
Bignor
Pulborough
West Sussex
RH20 1PH

 +44 (0)1798 869259

 Bignor Roman Villa

www.bignorromanvilla.co.uk

Transport links

Well signposted from the A29 Bury Road or the A285, south of Petworth

FISHBOURNE ROMAN PALACE

SITE LOCATION: FISHBOURNE, WEST SUSSEX

CONSTRUCTION DATE: C.AD43

SPECIAL FEATURES: ROMAN GARDENS

See map p.57 (7)

Fishbourne Palace was discovered as recently as the 1960s and nearly a decade's worth of subsequent excavations produced a series of remarkable finds.

Fishbourne appears to have been built as a military establishment soon after the Roman invasion of Britain in AD43, and then gradually to have developed into a luxurious palace over the succeeding century.

Some of Britain's finest mosaics — about 20 in all — are here, including the now famous 'Cupid on a Dolphin' which was made from a staggering 360,000 tiny pieces of mosaic or tesserae. This magnificent work of art forms part of the biggest collection of Roman mosaics in Britain that are still in the places for which they were originally created. All the mosaics are in what remains of the north wing of the palace.

Those interested in early gardens will be fascinated to discover that the original Roman gardens at Fishbourne have been recreated after meticulous archaeological research discovered the original layout and indications of the plants that were once grown here. In a small timber building nearby, a Roman gardener's toolshed has been reconstructed, using replica tools and some original implements excavated on the site.

Fishbourne is among the earliest of Britain's grand villas, dating from the middle of the 1st century, and completely justifies the use of the word 'palace'. The reception room would originally have been as much as 12 metres (40 feet) high and perhaps 40 metres (130 feet) long. Dozens of other equally impressive rooms were situated off a courtyard bounded by elegant columns. The plaster walls of the rooms would have been beautifully painted with scenes from mythology; and over 50 mosaics would have decorated the various chambers.

Evidence suggests that Fishbourne, though built and styled to a Mediterranean design, was actually the home of a 1st-century AD British king, most likely Cogidubnus, who ruled the Atrebates tribe and figures in the writings of the Roman historian Tacitus.

 Fishbourne boasts a delightful reconstruction of a Roman garden with a vine-clad pergola.

Fishbourne was destroyed by fire and then abandoned long before the Romans finally left Britain for good. Much of its stonework was plundered to construct other buildings, and during the succeeding centuries the site was used as a burial ground. However, despite the depredations of time and man, enough survives of what would once have been a beautiful building to make this one of Britain's great archaeological sites.

(i) information

Contact details

Fishbourne Roman Palace
Salthill Road, Fishbourne
Chichester, West Sussex
PO19 3QR

☎ +44 (0)1243 789829

📠 **Fishbourne site**
www.fishbourneromanpalace.com

Transport links

🚗 2.4 km (1½ miles) west of
Chichester. Signposted
from the A27 and A259

🚆 Fishbourne

🚌 Services 700, 56
and 11 stop near the
end of Salthill Road

LULLINGSTONE ROMAN VILLA

SITE LOCATION: SWANLEY, KENT
CONSTRUCTION DATE: c.AD75–410
SPECIAL FEATURES: WALL-PAINTING FRAGMENTS

See map p.57 **8**

Scholars had been aware of the existence of Lullingstone Roman Villa in Kent's Darenth Valley since the 18th century, when a mosaic pavement was uncovered. The full extent and importance of the villa itself were not fully appreciated until several decades later, when in 1939 archaeologists began to reveal one of the most important ancient sites in Britain.

The war slowed work to a halt but by 1949 excavations had shown that the site was well preserved and of great significance. It was taken into government control in 1958 and opened to the public in 1963.

▼ *Extensive foundations reveal much about Roman building techniques.*

Archaeologists believe that the villa was originally built in *c.*AD75 using timber, but by the middle of the 2nd century it had been rebuilt in stone. It was restored, extended and improved many times over the following centuries, until during the 5th century when it was almost destroyed by fire.

Some 26 rooms have been identified in the main part of the villa, along with four further rooms some distance from the main villa complex: a semicircular shrine, a kitchen, a mausoleum and a granary.

The Lullingstone site has yielded a wealth of treasures, including a mass of painted plaster fragments that have been reassembled to show just how beautifully the walls of the villa were once decorated.

The magnificent mosaic floor in the dining room has two main sections, both depicting scenes from Graeco–Roman mythology: the rape of Europa by Jupiter fills the semicircular end, while in the main area there is a wonderful portrayal

 A meticulous, if partial, reconstruction of decorated plaster found in the villa.

of Bellerophon killing the Chimera. A mass of skilfully executed geometric designs, including several swastikas – a common motif in Roman mosaics and architecture – decorate the area between the main panels. Visitors can also see some of the skeletons found at the site, together with the elaborate 4th-century bath complex.

(i) information

Contact details

Lullingstone Roman Villa
Lullingstone Lane
Eynsford, Kent
DA4 0JA

 +44 (0)1322 863467

 English Heritage site
www.english-heritage.org.uk
/daysout/properties
/lullingstone-roman-villa

Transport links

0.8 km (½ mile) south-west of Eynsford; Exit the M25 at junction 3 and take the A20 and then the A225

 Eynsford 1.2 km (¾ mile)

HOT BATH

DRAIN

HOT ROOM

ROMAN FLOOR LEVEL

WELWYN BATH HOUSE

SITE LOCATION: WELWYN, HERTFORDSHIRE   See map p.57 ⑨

CONSTRUCTION DATE: C.AD300

SPECIAL FEATURES: WELL-PRESERVED HYPOCAUST HEATING SYSTEM

One of the most interesting things about Welwyn Bath House is that you have to descend into a special chamber under a motorway to see it! The cost in time and money of leaving it in situ when the motorway – the A1(M) – was constructed above it is a tribute to an enlightened attitude to archaeological remains on the part of the authorities at the time. Although some would argue that it would have been far better to adjust the route of the road to leave the remains visible in the open air.

The bathhouse was originally part of a late Roman villa; it is well preserved and shows prime examples of the tepid, hot and cold baths that were so popular at the time.

The hypocaust heating system, which was so central a part of Roman villa building, is particularly well preserved at Welwyn Bath House. It relied on building the villa floor above stacks of tiles (each stack creating a tall pillar) to create a large space between the foundations of the villa and the underside of the floors. Into this space hot air was blown from a furnace area on the outside of one of the walls. At Welwyn, visitors can even see where the slaves would have been seated when stoking the fire.

◀ *The remains of the tepid, hot-and-cold baths favoured by the Romans are well preserved, as is the underfloor (hypocaust) heating system. The site also yielded fascinating artefacts which are on display.*

ⓘ information

Contact details

Welwyn Bath House
Welwyn Bypass Road
Welwyn, Hertfordshire
AL6 9FG

☎ +44 (0)1707 271362

 Welwyn Roman Baths site
www.welhat.gov.uk
/index.aspx?articleid=723

Transport links

 Welwyn North station,
2 km (1.3 miles)

 Services 00, 301 and 314

CHEDWORTH ROMAN VILLA

SITE LOCATION: CHEDWORTH, GLOUCESTERSHIRE   See map p.57 **10**
CONSTRUCTION DATE: c.AD100
SPECIAL FEATURES: ON-SITE MUSEUM

Chedworth is a large, well-preserved Roman villa with several superb mosaics, latrines, a water shrine, bathhouses and hypocausts. An on-site museum houses many of the fascinating objects that have been found during excavations over the years.

The villa may well have been sited here for the simple reason that water is readily available. Chedworth is the site of a natural spring that was channelled into a storage cistern, where a shrine was then constructed. Today, water from the spring still flows along the stone channel that was created by the Roman builders about 1,900 years ago.

Chedworth lasted a long time – about 400 years in all – and over that period grew from a relatively small and modest structure into a dwelling of great opulence – almost a miniature palace.

Originally consisting of three separate ranges of buildings (south, west and north), the villa appears to have been reasonably well established by AD150. The buildings dating from the earliest period seem to have been plain and functional, with no evidence of the grandeur apparent in the later additions, and the main accommodation was concentrated in the west range of the villa.

At some time in the 2nd century, a fire caused serious damage to the south and west ranges, but repairs appear to have been carried out immediately. At the same time as rebuilding was in progress, other improvements were made, including the addition of several rooms in the north range and an extension to the bath complex at its western end.

During the 4th century, a final major phase of expansion took place. In the early part of that century the Garden Court, an enclosed square completely surrounded by buildings, was created by extending the south and west ranges with additional rooms, effectively joining them at right angles. Open verandas were added around the inner perimeter of the three existing ranges, and a fourth was constructed midway along the south and north ranges to complete the enclosed quadrangle.

Also at this time, part of the existing bathhouse in the northern range was converted to a sauna, or dry heat bath,

 Well-preserved stone courses and mosaics make Chedworth Roman Villa in Gloucestershire one of Britain's most interesting archaeological sites.

and a new damp heat bath was added at the northern end of the west range.

Building work eventually came to an end late in the 4th century after a large dining room had been added at the eastern end of the north wing. With the completion of the four ranges and verandas, Chedworth Villa had been transformed from a simple dwelling into a luxurious house with a substantial bath complex.

ⓘ information

Contact details

Chedworth Roman Villa
Yanworth
Near Cheltenham
Gloucestershire
GL54 3LJ

 +44 (0)1242 890256

 National Trust site
www.nationaltrust.org.uk
/main/w-vh/w-visits
/w-findaplace
/w-chedworthromanvilla.htm

Transport links

 5 km (3 miles) north-west of Fossebridge on the A429

 Cheltenham Spa, 22.5 km (14 miles)

LETOCETUM

SITE LOCATION: WALL, STAFFORDSHIRE   See map p.57

CONSTRUCTION DATE: c.AD100

SPECIAL FEATURES: ON-SITE MUSEUM

Letocetum was a staging-post for couriers who travelled the Roman roads of Britain, which stretched from Hadrian's Wall in the north of England to the Roman port of Richborough in Kent. The name 'Letocetum' almost certainly derives from the Celtic *leito kaito*, meaning 'Grey Wood'.

Letocetum had a key position for the Romans as two major roads intersect nearby. Watling Street passed through the eastern gate of the staging-post and exited through the western fortifications, crossing the Icknield Way 0.8 kilometres (½ mile) away.

Evidence suggests that alongside the military settlement here, a Romano–British settlement grew up, covering as much as 12 hectares (30 acres), which probably traded with the soldiers.

The fort had impressive baths and would have provided accommodation for those travelling on official Roman business. The site was already important even before the arrival of the Romans as it lay on the boundary between the territories of two Celtic tribes – the Cronovii to the west and the Coritani to the east. It probably developed as a place where the two groups met to trade.

The remains of Letocetum today include Roman artefacts in the on-site museum, as well as the remains of an inn and a bathhouse.

 Letocetum would have been an important Roman trading post.

ⓘ information

Contact details

Letocetum
Watling Street, Wall
Lichfield, Staffordshire
WS14 0AW

 +44 (0)121 625 6820

 National Trust site
www.nationaltrust.org.uk
/main/w-wallromansite

Transport links

 Within the village of Wall, on the north side of the A5, 5 km (3 miles) south of Lichfield

WROXETER

SITE LOCATION: NEAR SHREWSBURY, SHROPSHIRE   See map p.57 (12)

CONSTRUCTION DATE: c.AD60–90

SPECIAL FEATURES: MUSEUM AND BATHHOUSE WALL

The Roman ruins at Wroxeter in the Midlands survive to a remarkable degree because the town was never developed to any great extent as a Saxon or medieval settlement. During the Roman occupation, however, it was the fourth biggest city in Britain (after London, Cirencester and St Albans), due to its position on the line of Watling Street, one of the Romans' most important routes across the country.

The first evidence of occupation at the site comes from about AD48, when the Fourteenth Legion was based here. In AD69, during the period when Wroxeter was still primarily a military fortress, it was followed by the Twentieth Legion. The surrounding settlement grew, inhabited largely by traders providing for the needs of the troops. When the soldiers left in AD80, the settlement became at first a *colonia* (a civic settlement for veterans) and then a tribal centre; the latter designation meant that it had its own administration and to some extent could run its own affairs.

Wroxeter was laid out according to the grid pattern common to most Roman settlements, including Silchester and Cirencester, with a range of civic buildings and a market at its heart. The most important of these to survive are the large public baths. Even today the great wall between the baths and exercise hall survives.

In the 2nd century, developments during the reign of the Emperor Hadrian included the addition of a basilica, as well as a new civic centre and bathhouse. The city's importance in the Roman Empire was reflected in a decision to improve its defences, and at the end of the 2nd century a 3.2-km (2-mile) long defensive ditch was dug around the perimeter. Decline set in during the 3rd and 4th centuries, when buildings fell into disrepair.

During the 5th century local tribal chiefs built new buildings along the existing Roman streets, but some time between 500 and 650 the city was finally abandoned.

Some of the most impressive Roman remains discovered in Britain can be seen at Wroxeter. A museum at the site includes excavated items and an audio tour of Roman life in Wroxeter's heyday.

▲ *The wall that divides the baths from the exercise hall still stands at Wroxeter (Roman name: Viroconium).*

ⓘ information

Contact details

Wroxeter
Shropshire
SY5 6PH

☎ +44 (0)1743 761330

 English Heritage site

www.english-heritage.org.uk
/daysout/properties
/wroxeter-roman-city

Transport links

 Located at Wroxeter, 8 km
(5 miles) east of Shrewsbury
on the B4380

 Shrewsbury, 9 km (5½ miles);
Wellington Telford West,
10 km (6 miles)

CHESTER ROMAN AMPHITHEATRE

SITE LOCATION: CHESTER, CHESHIRE

CONSTRUCTION DATE: c.1ST CENTURY AD

SPECIAL FEATURES: ARENA WALLS

See map p.57

Chester's splendid amphitheatre, built in the 1st century AD, was discovered quite by chance in 1929 during building work in the basement of a house. The intriguing remains that survive to this day include part of the western entrance, the arena walls and the arena itself, as well as the outer wall.

The amphitheatre originally had four entrances: two main entrances facing north and south, and two smaller entrances facing east and west. Between these entrances were smaller doorways that allowed access to a corridor running around the outside of the building and also to the staircases that led to the spectators' seats.

The amphitheatre was situated just outside the south-east corner of the legionary fortress overlooking the River Dee. It was most probably built in the 1st century, but archaeological evidence suggests that it was constructed on top of an even older amphitheatre.

This first amphitheatre may have been constructed in timber and only later rebuilt in stone or in a mix of stone and timber. By the middle of the 2nd century, the rebuilt amphitheatre was no longer in use; it had been allowed to fall into disrepair, and rubbish was piled up in the arena from about 150. However, in the late 3rd century, there was a revival of interest. There is evidence that the rubbish was cleared and repairs made to the arena, staircases and seats.

This phase of use lasted until the beginning of the 4th century, when the site again fell into disuse. The area around the amphitheatre was inhabited during the centuries following the Romans' departure, but was cleared during the English Civil War (1642–51) siege of Chester in 1645. Two Georgian houses were later built on the site: St John's House, constructed in the 1730s, was demolished to allow the northern part of the amphitheatre to be excavated, while Dee House, built over the southern half of the site, still stands.

 The extensive remains of Chester's once great amphitheatre. Part of the site is now hidden beneath 18th-century Dee House.

(i) information

Contact details

Chester Roman
Amphitheatre
Vicars Lane, Chester
Cheshire CH1 1QX

 English Heritage site

www.english-heritage.org.uk
/daysout/properties
/chester-roman-amphitheatre

Transport links

 On Vicars Lane, beyond
Newgate, Chester

Chester, 1.2 km (¾ mile)

YORK

SITE LOCATION: NORTH YORKSHIRE

CONSTRUCTION DATE: 1ST CENTURY AD

SPECIAL FEATURES: JORVIK VIKING CENTRE

See map p.57 (14)

York was founded by the Romans in the late 1st century at a strategically important spot where the River Foss met the River Ouse. The new settlement, called *Eboracum*, grew quickly at this vital crossing-point for goods, soldiers and civilians.

▼ *A Roman column re-erected outside York Minster.*

Today's city still bears traces of its Roman predecessor: sections its mainly medieval walls show signs of Roman work and excavations under its cathedral, York Minster, have revealed the Romans' military headquarters.

In 866, York become Jorvik when it was overrun by Viking invaders. The settlement they created overlays earlier remains, but much of what they submerged remained intact as the waterlogged soil conditions preserved masses of material that does not normally survive. This was first realized during the 1970s, when the area known as Coppergate underwent archaeological excavation and York became one of Britain's most important archaeological centres.

A 10th-century street was discovered, with the remains of houses and yards, latrines and workshops. There were extensive plant and animal remains, beautifully preserved fences, timber walls and other timber artefacts, leather goods and even clothing.

The huge number of finds and the quality of their preservation prompted

 Sections of York's city walls show signs of Roman work.

a decision to create the Jorvik Viking Centre, which recreates to a remarkable degree of accuracy a 10th-century Viking village. The archaeology here showed that these people were not warlike raiders of legend but – in York at least – settled residents who grew crops, built houses, reared animals and married local people.

information

Contact details

Jorvik Viking Centre
Coppergate, York
YO1 9WT

☎ +44 (0)1904 543400

 Jorvik Viking Centre site
www.jorvik-viking-centre.co.uk

Transport links

🚊 York

HADRIAN'S WALL

SITE LOCATION: NORTHUMBERLAND   See map p.57 (15)
CONSTRUCTION DATE: C.AD122
SPECIAL FEATURES: MILECASTLES, TEMPLES AND STONE COURSES

Hadrian's Wall is a physical reminder that there were places even the Romans could not conquer. The impossible terrain of Scotland, and the ferocity of its inhabitants, meant that keeping the barbarians out was easier than trying to bring them into the Roman fold.

For centuries after the Romans left, the wall was plundered by local farmers and road builders, and though today it is visible for much of its length, it is nowhere higher than about 1 metre (3 feet). When first built, the wall would have been over 6 metres (20 feet) high with milecastles, turrets and forts dotted along its 80 Roman miles (120 kilometres/73 miles).

Roman Emperor Hadrian (r. 117–138) who arrived in Britain in AD122, ordered the wall to be built – probably by legionnaires rather than slaves. Large forts were built at intervals and were part military camp and part civilian settlement, with houses, grain stores, baths and so on. The milecastles (as the name suggests, they were built at every mile) would each have had a

▼ *The wild and lonely miles of Hadrian's Wall, near Hotbank Crags.*

garrison of eight soldiers. Between each milecastle were two watchtowers, manned by two soldiers.

The wall, designated a World Heritage Site in 1987, runs from Bowness-on-Solway in Cumbria in the west to Wallsend in Tyne and Wear in the east. There are various sites of interest along it. In Northumberland, at Chesters Roman Fort are large numbers of Roman artefacts collected by the Victorian antiquary John Clayton. At the fort, almost certainly a cavalry garrison, the Roman lavatory system is still clearly visible. There are also the remains of a Roman bridge here, which would have spanned the River Tyne.

The best-preserved stretch of the wall begins in Northumberland at Sewingshields Farm. Here, it runs for hundreds of metres across the dramatic landscape of Whin Sill.

At Sewingshields Milecastle, there is an extraordinary feature – a Saxon grave built right up against the wall for reasons that we are never likely to discover. Nothing else like it exists in the world. At Knag Burn, you can see not only the wall stretching away but also a Roman gateway, still with its two guardrooms.

Housesteads, an extraordinarily well-preserved fort, comes next. The Romans called it *Vercovicium*. It covers 2 hectares (5 acres) and originally included a granary, hospital, latrines and barracks. Near Peel Crags, a swastika – a common motif in Roman designs – can be seen carved into a stone in one of the lower courses.

At Carlisle, the Tullie House Museum boasts a collection of Roman artefacts and galleries about Hadrian's Wall.

ⓘ information

Contact details

Hadrian's Wall 135-km (84-mile) signposted trail from coast to coast, Wallsend in the east to Bowness-on-Solway in the west

🖳 **Hadrian's Wall site**
www.hadrians-wall.org

🖳 **Tullie House Museum site**
www.tulliehouse.co.uk

Transport links

🚗 The A69 between Newcastle and Carlisle runs parallel to Hadrian's Wall for about 3–8 km (2–5 miles) and is the main access route. The M6, A74(M) and A1(M) also pass near to the wall

 Trains from Newcastle and Carlisle run directly into Hadrian's Wall country

BLACKSTONE EDGE ROMAN ROAD

SITE LOCATION: NEAR ROCHDALE, LANCASHIRE   See map p.57

CONSTRUCTION DATE: UNKNOWN

SPECIAL FEATURES: STONE GULLEYS

Arguments have raged for decades about the apparently ancient, skilfully made stone surfaced road that crosses remote Blackstone Edge near Littleborough on the edge of the Pennines mountain range.

Some experts have argued that the road is a medieval packhorse route. Others insist it is a remnant of a true Roman road. Archaeologists are still in disagreement, but there is no doubt that the road is very old, and it does bear a remarkable resemblance in terms of construction to many Roman roads. It has typical stone ribs, for example, and a deep central drainage channel. Between sturdy kerbs lie beautifully tooled cobbles that have been cut and fitted with precision.

The central gulley is designed to ensure that rainfall on the road dispersed quickly, greatly assisted by the camber and side gulleys. Remarkably, the road is nearly 6 metres (20 feet) wide in some places. Those who favour the Roman theory argue that the Blackstone Edge road ran from Manchester (*Mancunium*) to Ilkley (*Verbeia*).

 Blackstone Edge Roman Road is skilfully made from precisely cut stones.

(i) information

Contact details

Blackstone Edge
Roman Road
Rishworth Moor
Pennines

 Roman Roads site
www.historic-uk.com
/HistoryUK/England-History
/RomanRoads.htm

Transport links

On the A 672, by junction 22 of the M62

RIBCHESTER ROMAN FORT

SITE LOCATION: **NEAR BLACKBURN, LANCASHIRE**   See map p.57

CONSTRUCTION DATE: c.AD78–200

SPECIAL FEATURES: **NEARBY ROMAN MUSEUM**

What we call Ribchester Fort today was known to the Romans as *Bremetonaci* or *Bremetenacum Veteranorum*.

The fort covered 2 hectares (5 acres) and was protected by a 6-metre (20-feet) wide double ditch and rampart. Originally it was built entirely from timber, and in this form was probably complete by about AD78.

By this time, there was a bathhouse and at least one temple outside the defences. Spanish and Hungarian 'Roman' units were based here and there was even a hall built specifically for cavalry practice. A bronze cavalry helmet is among the fascinating artefacts discovered at this site. The fort and temples were completely destroyed in AD301–306, but the latest coin and pottery evidence for activity here comes from the late 4th century.

Evidence suggests that the inhabitants of the fort were usually well fed – bones from red and roe deer, goose and swan have been uncovered, and there was a double granary, together with latrines, and altars.

Ribchester now has a Roman museum that houses a wonderful collection of objects found in and around the Roman fort. These discoveries even include some timber and leather artefacts, in addition to coins, carved stone and metalwork items. The museum's collection also includes a number of splendid sculptures and funeral monuments.

 Ribchester is rich in fascinating remains, including stone courses, pillars and superb carvings.

(i) information

Contact details

Ribchester Roman Museum
Riverside, Ribchester
Preston, Lancashire, PR3 3XS

 +44 (0)1254 878261

 **Roman Museum site**
www.ribchesterromanmuseum.org

Transport links

 15 minutes from junction 31 of the M6

HARDKNOTT ROMAN FORT

SITE LOCATION: NEAR ESKDALE, CUMBRIA   See map p.57 **(18)**
CONSTRUCTION DATE: c.AD120-130
SPECIAL FEATURES: REMOTE AND BEAUTIFUL LOCATION

In the wild remote hills of Cumbria, a hectare (2½ acres) of land was once home to the Roman fort of *Mediobogdum*, or Hardknott Fort as it is now known. The Romans occupied this region for about 350 years and *Mediobogdum* would have held about 500 soldiers, who guarded the road between the forts at Ravenglass and Ambleside.

Now managed by English Heritage, the fort was probably built between AD120 and 130, and the well-preserved remains include granaries, barracks, the commandant's headquarters and baths. An area of flattened ground is thought to be the parade area.

Perhaps most impressive of all are the extraordinarily beautiful views from the Eskdale end of Hardknott Pass – delightful now from an aesthetic perspective, but also a reminder of why the fort was built here: the commanding position gave the defenders plenty of notice of any hostile army.

Despite the fact that this fort was remote from the great centres of Roman occupation, it is worth remembering that it was part of a network of forts, towns and other outposts that were kept in regular contact with each other via the Romans' splendid network of roads and communications systems.

The spectacular hilly backdrop of Hardknott Roman Fort. This fort would have been a remote outpost of the ▶ *Roman Empire almost 2,000 years ago – just as remote then as it is today.*

 information

Contact details

Hardknott Roman Fort
Near Eskdale
Lake District
Cumbria

 English Heritage site
www.english-heritage.org.uk
/daysout/properties
/hardknott-roman-fort

Transport links

 14.5 km (9 miles) north-east of Ravenglass

 Dalegarth, 5 km (3 miles); Ravenglass 16 km (10 miles)

94 RAVENGLASS

SITE LOCATION: CUMBRIA

CONSTRUCTION DATE: c.1ST CENTURY AD

SPECIAL FEATURES: BATHHOUSE WALLS

See map p.57 **19**

The remains of the Roman fort of *Glannaventa* stand at Ravenglass on the west coast of Cumbria, where the Rivers Irt, Esk and Mite converge. The well-watered nature of the site no doubt lay behind the Romans' decision to build their defensive position here. *Glannoventa* would have provided a good anchorage for Roman boats pulled up on the shallow curving banks of the river estuary, well protected from storms. It was an important naval base for the Romans. Little remains of the original fort apart from the bathhouse, which is actually situated outside the fort itself. Its well-preserved walls still stand to a height of 3 metres (12 feet) and follow a zig-zag plan. Their fine, round-topped arches and beautifully cut facing stones can still be seen.

The remains of the Roman bathhouse have been dated to the 1st century AD. A museum at the site contains a remarkable find: a Roman soldier's bronze diploma, granting discharge from the army, dated 27 February 158.

Lead seals have also been unearthed over the years, and these suggest that the First Cohort of the Aelian Fleet was based here. The Fleet was a part of the *Classis Britannica* (British naval fleet).

It is important to remember that Roman soldiers were not necessarily 'Roman' at all — they might be Spanish, or from Gaul or any other part of the Roman Empire.

◀ *This fine round-topped arch at Ravenglass may have been a shrine niche.*

▲ *The walls of the Roman bathhouse at Ravenglass survive to a height of 3 metres (12 feet).*

ⓘ information

Contact details

Ravenglass
Cumbria
CA18 1RW

🌐 **English Heritage site**

www.english-heritage.org.uk
/daysout/properties
/ravenglass-roman-
bath-house

Transport links

 0.4 km (¼ mile) east
of Ravenglass

 Whitehaven–Millom
service 6 or X6

 Ravenglass

DOLAUCOTHI GOLD MINE

SITE LOCATION: CARMARTHENSHIRE, WALES   See map p.57 **20**
CONSTRUCTION DATE: c.AD75
SPECIAL FEATURES: WORKINGS FROM VARIOUS PERIODS

Gold has been mined at Dolaucothi since Roman times. The mine itself is now owned by the National Trust and two of the old underground workings are open to visitors.

The Romans were certainly mining gold here by AD75, but there is evidence that earlier people also came here for the valuable metal. Some archaeological evidence points to mining as far back as the 6th century BC or earlier.

With the departure of the Romans, the mine seems to have been largely abandoned for 1,000 years or more, although there is evidence of some mining before the major resurgence of interest in the 19th century – particularly in what are known as the Upper and Lower Roman adits, or horizontal shafts, which are not Roman despite their names.

During the 1930s, gold to the value of just over £11,000 a year was extracted; but by the end this decade the cost and difficulty of extracting the gold from the surrounding rock made the mine uneconomic.

Today the site is a fascinating reminder of how ancient mining was conducted. Visitors can see many of the artefacts discovered here and learn about the techniques employed by Roman and other early gold miners.

 *Roman horizontal shafts and more recent workings make Dolaucothi's archaeology particularly interesting.*

ⓘ information

Contact details

Dolaucothi Gold Mines
Pumsaint, Llanwrda
Carmarthenshire
SA19 8US

☎ +44 (0)1558 650177

 National Trust site
www.nationaltrust.org.uk
/main/w-dolaucothigoldmines

Transport links

 Between Lampeter
and Llanwrda on the A482

 Service 289 from
Lampeter

 Llanwrda, 13 km (8 miles)

EARLY MEDIEVAL PERIOD

AD411–1066

After the departure of the Romans in the early 5th century AD, Britain was long supposed to have descended into a period of ignorance and barbarity – 'The Dark Ages'. This view has now been largely revised, and the achievements of the invaders from Northern Europe can be seen for what they really are. The Vikings and Saxons that settled in Britain built farms, villages, halls and towns, but the great tradition among these people was to build in timber, and timber only rarely survives. That said, there are several wonderful archaeological sites from the period between the departure of the Romans and the coming of the Normans in 1066. These sites include the Balladoole Viking Ship Burial in the Isle of Man and the numerous Saxon churches and chapels dotted around the country.

EARLY MEDIEVAL LOCATIONS

1. Glastonbury Abbey
2. Corfe Castle
3. St Peter-on-the-Wall
4. St Andrew's Church, Greensted
5. West Stow
6. Church of St Mary and Odda's Chapel, Deerhurst
7. St Peter's Church, Barton-on-Humber
8. Lindisfarne
9. Balladoole Viking Ship Burial
10. Iona
11. Nendrum Monastery

Shetland Islands

Inverness
Aberdeen

(10)

EDINBURGH
Glasgow
(8)

Newcastle upon tyne

Londonderry
Donegal
NORTHERN
IRELAND
BELFAST
(11)

(9)

York
(7)

IRELAND
Galway
DUBLIN

Liverpool
Manchester

Caernarfon

Limerick

ENGLAND
Norwich

Waterford

Birmingham
(5)
Cambridge

Killarney

WALES
Oxford
(3)

CARDIFF
Bristol
(6)
LONDON
(4)

(1)
Southampton
Dover

Exeter
(2)
Brighton

GLASTONBURY ABBEY

100

SITE LOCATION: GLASTONBURY, SOMERSET See map p.99
CONSTRUCTION DATE: c.10TH–16TH CENTURY AD
SPECIAL FEATURES: ROMANTIC RUINS

The site of the abbey has been inhabited since ancient times; but stories about the legendary King Arthur and the Knights of the Round Table have always confused history with mythology.

Ine, the local Saxon king of Wessex in the 8th century, is said to have built the first stone church here and its base is believed to form the foundation of the west end of the current nave. Legend has it that King Arthur is buried here, despite the fact that there is no firm proof he even existed.

The history of Glastonbury becomes easier to untangle when we contemplate the remains we see today. In the 900s, the abbot of Glastonbury, St Dunstan, who was to become Archbishop of Canterbury in 960, began to enlarge the original church. This rebuilding continued when the Normans took over after 1066; then disaster struck in 1184, when the monastery was badly damaged by fire. Yet by 1213, with that great spirit of eternal optimism that characterizes medieval builders, the work of rebuilding had finished and a fine new church had risen from the ashes of the old.

Further building work was carried out in the 14th century, the period of the abbey's greatest wealth – a time when Glastonbury was one of the biggest landowners in Wessex and able to wield significant political and religious power. The abbey kitchen that survives today dates from this period. Early records about the abbey and how it was built are extensive – we know, for example, that the kitchen was part of the magnificent abbot's house built between 1334 and 1342 by then-abbot John de Breynton.

Archaeology has revealed some fascinating facts about Glastonbury. For example, the highest-ranking pilgrims might once have stayed in the abbey itself, as is suggested by excavations that have disclosed a special apartment at the south end of the abbot's house. It is believed that this was built for a visit from Henry VII (r. 1485–1509).

In 1536, the heyday of Glastonbury Abbey came to an end with the closure, pillage and large-scale destruction that followed the Dissolution of the Monasteries, brought about by Henry VIII (r. 1509–47).

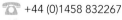 *Despite the destruction caused by the Reformation, Glastonbury's former architectural greatness can still be seen in its ruins.*

ⓘ information

Contact details

Glastonbury Abbey
The Abbey Gatehouse
Magdalene Street
Glastonbury, Somerset
BA6 9EL

☎ +44 (0)1458 832267

Glastonbury Abbey

www.glastonburyabbey.com

Transport links

From the M5, take junction 23 and follow signs to Glastonbury

Castle Cary, 24 km (15 miles)

Service 376 from Bristol; service 29 from Taunton

CORFE CASTLE

SITE LOCATION:	NEAR WAREHAM, DORSET	See map p.99 ②
CONSTRUCTION DATE:	C.EARLY 12TH CENTURY AD	
SPECIAL FEATURES:	FINE NORMAN ARCHITECTURE	

Corfe Castle sits high on a site that has been strategically important since Norman times or earlier, for it controls a pass in the Purbeck Hills on the route linking coastal Swanage to inland Wareham, both situated in Dorset. The first castle here, which was completed in the 9th century, was probably a timber construction.

The later motte castle (a castle built on a mound) was made from local Purbeck stone. Its keep was completed in 1106, during the reign of Henry I (r. 1100–35).

▼ *Now in ruins, Corfe Castle was once of great strategic significance.*

In the 13th century, its defences were strengthened with a stone curtain wall and stone towers, probably completed by 1285. Corfe Castle remained a royal residence until sold by Elizabeth I (r. 1558–1603) in the 16th century.

The current majestic ruins are all that remain of this later building, after it was destroyed during the English Civil War (1642–51). Then owned by Sir John Bankes, Attorney General to Charles I (r. 1629–45), the castle was besieged by Parliamentary forces for several years. An act of treachery among the inhabitants of the castle led to its downfall in 1646. After which, it was 'slighted' – badly damaged, if not quite taken down stone by stone. However, many fine Norman and Early English architectural and archaeological features of the castle remain to this day.

The Parliamentary forces were so impressed by the fortitude of Sir John Bankes's wife, Lady Bankes, who had held out so long against them, that she was allowed to leave in peace and carrying the castle keys. Others who defended the castle during Lady Bankes's tenure and were not of aristocratic birth were not treated so leniently. Many were hanged.

As with many ancient castles, Corfe crops up in several stories. Some recall events that really happened; others are more fanciful. Edward the Martyr, eldest son of King Edgar (r. 959–75), was certainly assassinated at the castle gates in 978, aged just 16. The event is recorded in the *Anglo–Saxon Chronicle*. And in 1202, King John (r.1199–1216) is said to have imprisoned some 22 noblemen in Corfe Castle and allowed them to starve to death.

 ## information

Contact details

Corfe Castle
Wareham
Dorset
BH20 5EZ

☎ +44 (0)1929 481294

 National Trust site
www.nationaltrust.org.uk
/main/w-corfecastle

Transport links

 Situated on the A351 Wareham–Swanage road

 Service 40 on the Poole–Swanage route

 Wareham, 7.2 km (4½ miles); Corfe Castle, on the Swanage–Norden steam railway line

ST PETER-ON-THE-WALL

SITE LOCATION: BRADWELL-ON-SEA, ESSEX   See map p.99 **3**
CONSTRUCTION DATE: C.AD650
SPECIAL FEATURES: REMOTE LOCATION

If there were a prize for the loneliest-seeming building in the British Isles, then St Peter-on-the-Wall in deepest Essex would surely be a contender.

Several kilometres from any house, St Peter-on-the-Wall stands at the mouth of the River Blackwater. It was built by St Cedd in the 650s, using stone and brick from a nearby Roman fort, Othona, that might well – just 200 years after the Romans left Britain – have still been largely intact at the time building work on the church began. All that remains today is the chapel. This would once have been just one part of a small group of monastic buildings.

When the wind hurtles in from the North Sea, this is a bitter place. However, St Cedd had travelled to Essex from the monastery of Lindisfarne on the cold and windswept northeastern coast of Northumberland. So this wild place would have felt like home to him.

Even today there is a long walk from the nearest road to reach the chapel, but this is part of its charm. Little is left inside to tell of its extraordinary 1,400-year life, but the fact that it was used as a barn from the 14th century is probably the only reason the building survived at all. In the 1920s it was finally restored to its former glory as a chapel.

◀ *St Peter-on-the-Wall probably only survived because it made a useful barn. It almost certainly uses materials recycled from Othona, the Roman fort, that once stood nearby.*

ⓘ information

Contact details

Chapel of St Peter-on-the-Wall
Bradwell-on-Sea
Essex

 +44 (0)1621 776203

 Chapel of St Peter-on-the-Wall
www.bradwellchapel.org

Transport links

 From the A130, head towards South Woodham Ferrers and continue onto Bradwell-on-Sea

ST ANDREW'S CHURCH, GREENSTED

SITE LOCATION: ESSEX
CONSTRUCTION DATE: C.AD650
SPECIAL FEATURES: OLDEST TIMBER CHURCH IN THE WORLD

See map p.99

Just outside Chipping Ongar in Essex, and concealed down an unlikely-looking track, stands what is almost certainly the oldest wooden church in the world. Timber, the favoured building material of Vikings and Saxons does not last — which explains why we know far more about the architecture of the Romans, who built largely in stone, in Britain than about the timber-building invaders of the so-called 'Dark Ages'.

The walls of this church, St Andrew's, Greensted, are made from whole split-oak tree trunks probably positioned there in the 11th century. The curved side of each split log faces outward, leaving the flat sides to create a mor-or-less even surface on the inside of the church. The Normans and Tudors added to the church and it has been restored many times, but for some extraordinary reason the oak walls were never replaced.

Traces of earlier churches have been discovered beneath the present building. The earliest structure was probably completed several centuries before the current building — as far back as AD650. The Saxon builders set upright timbers in a trench in the ground to give the building sufficient rigidity. However, because the ends of the massive posts stood in damp ground they soon rotted away.

The 11th-century rebuild involved a clever new design that would eliminate the problem of timbers having to be set in the ground. The timber walls of the new church were slotted into a massive wall plate — a timber running along the ground horizontally. Despite this innovation, by the mid-19th century the bottoms of the wall timbers had rotted so the decayed sections were removed and the timbers repositioned but this time on top of a low-built brick wall.

What makes the timber walls of this church particularly fascinating is that the marks of the carpenters — the distinctive cuts made using an adze — can still be seen on the inner surfaces of the split timbers.

▲ *The walls of St Andrew's Church, Greensted, are made from whole split-oak trunks that were fashioned in Saxon times.*

ⓘ information

Contact details

St Andrews Church
Church Lane
Greensted Road
Greensted
Essex, CM5 9LA

☎ +44 (0)1277 363268

www Greensted Church
www.greenstedchurch.org.uk

Transport links

🚗 From the M25 or M11, follow signs to the A414 and then signs to Greensted

🚆 Epping Underground and Brentwood, both 11.3 km (7 miles)

WEST STOW

SITE LOCATION: NEAR MILDENHALL, SUFFOLK   See map p.99 **5**

CONSTRUCTION DATE: PRE-AD650

SPECIAL FEATURES: RECONSTRUCTED SAXON HOUSES

West Stow in Suffolk reveals a wealth of evidence of continuous habitation from Neolithic times (4000–2500BC) right through the Roman period (AD43–410) in Britain. The earliest evidence comes in the form of beautifully crafted flint tools, but we know that there was an Iron Age fort here and there is also evidence of

▼ *A careful study of preserved remains at West Stow has allowed archaeologists to reconstruct a Saxon house.*

Romano–British occupation in the form of pottery remains. Following the departure of the Romans, an Anglo–Saxon settlement developed here. The site was abandoned in about AD650 and the village moved further up the River Lark. Soon after this, the remains of the settlement would have been buried, and though the land was used for agriculture the remains of the Saxon village were protected by enough sand and soil to preserve it. In 1972, the long-lost village was rediscovered by archaeologists.

By then, Suffolk had long been known to be rich in Anglo–Saxon remains, so it was perhaps no great surprise to find a major settlement here. Nevertheless, the discovery was particularly exciting because the sand had preserved plenty of organic material. This meant that archaeologists could make accurate assessments of the inhabitants' diet and the textiles they used.

Modern but accurate reconstructions of the houses that once stood here are revealing. There was no focal point to the village and no coherent street system in the modern sense; instead, the houses seem to have been scattered randomly. When they died, the inhabitants were buried with their possessions, a practice revealing them still to have been pagans.

West Stow also provided some new information about our Saxon forebears: for example, their huts may have had suspended timber floors with cellars beneath. Other finds include quern stones – used for grinding flour – and large quantities of cattle, sheep and pig bones.

Two of the ancient timber houses had been burned rather than abandoned, leaving archaeologists a greater wealth of preserved remains (charred timber is resistant to rot) than would normally be found at such a site.

information

Contact details

West Stow
The Visitor Centre
Icklingham Road
West Stow, Bury St Edmunds
Suffolk, IP28 6HG

 +44 (0) 1284 728718

 West Stow

www.stedmundsbury.gov.uk
/sebc/play/weststow-asv.cfm

Transport links

 11.3 km (7 miles) north-west of Bury St Edmunds, off the A1101

CHURCH OF ST MARY AND ODDA'S CHAPEL, DEERHURST

SITE LOCATION: **GLOUCESTERSHIRE**   See map p.99 **6**
CONSTRUCTION DATE: C.AD804
SPECIAL FEATURES: **SAXON INSCRIBED STONE**

The village of Deerhurst, in Gloucestershire, is very rare in having two Saxon buildings: the Church of St Mary and Odda's Chapel.

The church with its large distinctive tower looks later medieval or Tudor from a distance but up close it is quickly apparent from the decorative features that it is Saxon. The church and nearby farmhouse were almost certainly once part of a monastery. The tower has distinctive herringbone masonry and curious animal-head carvings. The first record of this church comes from 804, but the earliest, rectangular part of the building was probably started in the late 600s.

The polygonal apse and chapels are thought to be 9th century, and the porch 10th century. There are pointed saxon windows, a small saxon doorway and stained glass dating from about 1300.

Just down the road is Odda's Chapel. Now part of a medieval farmhouse, the chapel is tiny with just two rooms but still has its original window openings and chancel arch. An inscription on a stone found nearby in the 17th century reveals that:

'Earl Odda had this royal hall built and dedicated in honour of the Holy Trinity for the soul of his brother Aelfric.'

The Saxon tower of the Church of St Mary in Deerhurst has distinctive masonry details and curious carvings. ▶

ⓘ information

Contact details

Church of St Mary
   and Odda's Chapel
Deerhurst
Gloucestershire
GL19 4BX

 Church of St Mary
www.deerhurstfriends.co.uk

English Heritage site
www.english-heritage.org.uk
/daysout/properties/oddas-chapel

Transport links

 5 km (3 miles) south of Tewkesbury on the A38 towards Gloucester. Turn west onto the B4213 and follow signs to Deerhurst

ST PETER'S CHURCH, BARTON-UPON-HUMBER

SITE LOCATION: NORTH LINCOLNSHIRE   See map p.99 (7)
CONSTRUCTION DATE: LATE 10TH CENTURY AD
SPECIAL FEATURES: SAXON BAPTISTRY

The most extraordinary feature of St Peter's Church in North Lincolnshire is its west tower, which dates from the late Saxon and early Norman periods, and its unique annex, which is the only surviving Saxon baptistry in the country.

Research suggests that the first church, built in the late 900s, was constructed on an older cemetery. About a century later, that church was demolished, but leaving the tower and its western annex. The new church, built around the existing tower and annex, included a nave, sanctuary and chancel. By 1200, those buildings had been replaced by a new church. In the 1200s, the south aisle, porch and chancel were demolished, and the wider aisle and larger porch were constructed.

Excavation revealed an astonishing 2,836 graves below the church and in the churchyard. Very early timber coffins were preserved in some parts of the waterlogged ground – a rare occurrence and invaluable for archaeologists – and in one coffin the skeleton of a presumed bishop was discovered still with his crozier.

 There have been some wonderful archaeological finds at St Peter's, which can be seen in a permanent exhibition set up by English Heritage.

(i) information

Contact details

St Peter's Church,
Barton-upon-Humber
North Lincolnshire
DN18 5EX

☎ +44 (0)1652 632516

[www] **English Heritage site**
www.english-heritage.org.uk
/daysout/properties/st-peters-
church-barton-upon-humber

Transport links

 Hull–Scunthorpe
service 350

 Barton-upon-Humber,
0.8 km (½ mile)

114

LINDISFARNE

SITE LOCATION: **NORTHUMBERLAND**   See map p.99 **8**
CONSTRUCTION DATE: **c.13TH CENTURY AD**
SPECIAL FEATURES: **MONASTERY RUINS AND 18TH-CENTURY CASTLE**

For many, Lindisfarne Island – or Holy Island, as it is also known – off the coast of Northumberland is the most important Christian site of Anglo– Saxon England. The windswept causeway is passable on foot only when the tide is at its lowest, twice each day. The rest of the time the island is cut off by fierce currents as the sea sweeps in across the tidal causeway.

The monastery at Lindisfarne was founded in AD635 by Aidan, an Irish monk from Iona, a small island off the coast of Scotland, who was asked by King Oswald of Northumbria to convert his kingdom to the new religion. The 7th century saw the making here of one of the greatest of all medieval works of art, the Lindisfarne Gospels, and the tenure of Lindisfarne's greatest bishop, St Cuthbert, who died in AD687.

By the end of the 8th century, Viking raids forced the monks to leave. The monastery was re-established in the 12th century and monks remained the until the Dissolution of the Monasteries in 1536.

The monastic remains date from the 13th century, but the original monastery was founded in 635. ▶

 ## information

Contact details

The Holy Island
  of Lindisfarne
Northumberland
TD15 2SH

 +44 (0)1289 389244

 The Holy Island of Lindisfarne
www.lindisfarne.org.uk

Transport links

 Service 477 from Berwick-upon-Tweed, with connecting buses at Beal to and from Newcastle. Services vary with season and tides

 On Holy Island, 8 km (5 miles) east of the A1

 Berwick-upon-Tweed, 16 km (10 miles)

BALLADOOLE VIKING SHIP BURIAL

SITE LOCATION:	ISLE OF MAN	See map p.99 (9)
CONSTRUCTION DATE:	C.AD 900	
SPECIAL FEATURES:	REMOTE LOCATION	

The ship burial at Balladoole's Chapel Hill on the Isle of Man dates back to c.AD900. By any standards, the Balladoole Viking Ship Burial is impressive. The vessel closely resembles known examples of similar ships: originally it would have been roughly 11 to 14 metres (36–40 feet) long and 4 metres (11 feet) at its widest part, or beam.

The size of the ship and the quality of the grave goods found in it suggest that the man for whom the burial was made was important. His remains were discovered in the centre of the boat; with him were found a knife, flints, a belt buckle, a ringed pin, a horse's bit, spurs and a cauldron, as well as remains of clothing, tools and a shield. Whomever he was, he was almost certainly buried in a fine-quality linen garment of some kind.

The belt-buckle design has much in common with similar items from the Dublin area of Ireland and from the Isle of Lewis, which hints at the link between cultures across and around the Irish Sea at this time. During the Viking period, the Isle of Man was at the centre of a number of important sea routes criss-crossing between the Scottish islands, Ireland, England and Scandinavia. In addition, the range of goods found in the ship burial at Balladoole reflects this network of communication and trade. The design of the spurs suggests a continental origin. The absence of a sword is unusual but could be the result of early grave robbers.

A woman found buried alongside the man had no accompanying grave goods and her remains are incomplete. This may indicate that she was a sacrificial victim (such sacrifices have been noted in other, similar graves).

Curiously, the burial took place in an area of early Christian graves. This may have been the Vikings' way of expressing their control or domination over the local Christian people, or it may possibly be a sign that the Viking and Celtic cultures were beginning to merge.

 The position of the Balladoole Viking ship burial can be seen marked clearly by white stones.

ⓘ information

Contact details

Balladoole Viking
Ship Burial
Near Castletown
Isle of Man

🌐 **Balladoole Burial**

www.iomguide.com
/balladoole.php

Transport links

🚌 Services 1, 1C, 2 and 2C
stop about 0.8 km (½ mile)
from the burial site

🚗 On the A5 between
Castletown and Port St
Mary. Take side road off the
A5, heading to Balladoole

🚆 From Douglas, take
the steam-railway line
to Castletown, which is
about 2.5 km (1½ miles)
from the burial site

IONA

SITE LOCATION: NEAR ISLE OF MULL, SCOTLAND   See map p.99 **10**
CONSTRUCTION DATE: C.13TH CENTURY AD
SPECIAL FEATURES: CELTIC CROSSES

Christianity in Britain began on the tiny island of Iona, off the coast of Scotland. St Columba, an Irish monk, arrived here in AD563 to establish a monastic community. So successful was he in converting the Scots and northern English to Christianity that Iona soon became well-known throughout Christian Europe. In time, Columba built an abbey on Iona, and is famous (or infamous) for banning cows and women from the island on the grounds that they caused mischief.

The monastery at Iona is widely known for its stone crosses and illuminated manuscripts, including one of the greatest surviving works of art of the middle ages, the *Book of Kells*, which contains the four Gospels and was made here in about AD800.

Nothing of St Columba's first chapel survives. Legend has it that the saint is buried beside the abbey. From the 9th to 12th centuries, the island was subjected to Viking raids. In 1203, the Order of Black Nuns established themselves on the island and the present Benedictine abbey was built. It was destroyed in the Scottish Reformation of 1560 but restored in the 20th century.

◀ *A Celtic cross is a reminder of the distinct form of Christianity that once existed on Iona.*

ⓘ information

Contact details

Iona
Near Isle of Mull
Scotland

☎ +44 (0)1681 700512

 Historic Scotland site
www.historic-scotland.gov.uk
/propertyresults
/propertyoverview.htm
?PropID=PL_160&PropName
=IonaAbbeyAndNunnery

Transport links

 From Oban, take the ferry to Craignure on Mull; from Craignure, take the 496 bus to Fionnphort ferry terminal; and from Fionnphort, take the ferry to Iona

NENDRUM MONASTERY

SITE LOCATION: COMBER, NORTHERN IRELAND   See map p.99 (11)
CONSTRUCTION DATE: C.5TH CENTURY AD
SPECIAL FEATURES: ROUND TOWER AND SUNDIAL

Mahee Island, in Ireland's vast inland water Strangford Lough, can be reached by a causeway today, but more than 1,500 years ago this would have been a very remote and inaccessible spot.

Today, visitors are attracted by the substantial remains of the monastery, which thrived until Viking raids in the second half of the 10th century. The site was finally destroyed in AD976 by a fire, which is said to have killed the abbot.

An important pre-Norman monastery, Nendrum had three concentric stone-wall enclosures. All are still clearly visible, together with a ruined church, the foundations of a typical Irish round tower, workshops, huts, a graveyard, a tidal mill, a number of cross slabs and a sundial.

By the 12th century, a small Benedictine community had been established where the monastery had once been. Abandoned once again in the 15th century, Nendrum lay undiscovered until the mid-19th century.

Nendrum's remote location is typical of early Celtic monastic foundations. Away from the temptations of the world, the monks felt that they could contemplate God with fewer distractions. However, their isolation meant that the monastic community had to be largely self-sufficient.

The foundations of a typical Irish round tower and a section of one of Nendrum's three enclosing stone walls. ▶

ⓘ information

Contact details

Nendrum Monastery
Mahee Island
Comber, County Down
Northern Ireland

 +44 (0)28 9054 3037

 Saint Patrick's Trail
www.discovernorthernireland.com
/Nendrum-Monastic-Site-Comber-
Newtownards-P2877

Transport links

 From Belfast, take the A20 towards Newtownards until the intersection with the A22. Take the A22, through Comber, and follow the signs for Mahee Island

LATE MEDIEVAL PERIOD

AD 1067–1485

Immediately after the Norman Conquest, William I (r. 1066–87) set about consolidating his power in England. He built castles across the land, a remarkable number of which survive relatively intact to this day – most famously the White Tower at the Tower of London and Conwy Castle on the Welsh border. With military power established, the next great programme of building could begin, driven by the Christian Church. Monastic buildings of unimaginable splendour grew up in many places the length and breadth of the country. As well as the monasteries and churches, great medieval timber barns survive from this period, along with remote country houses and splendid fortified manors.

LATE MEDIEVAL LOCATIONS

1. Cerne Abbas Giant
2. Lacock Abbey
3. Malmesbury Abbey
4. St Botolph's, Hardham
5. Winchelsea
6. Dover Castle
7. Cressing Temple Barns
8. Tower of London
9. St Oswald's, Widford
10. Kenilworth Castle
11. Stokesay Castle
12. Little Moreton Hall
13. Rievaulx Abbey
14. Furness Abbey
15. Conwy Castle
16. St David's Cathedral
17. Melrose Abbey
18. Caerlaverock Castle
19. Dunluce
20. Clonmacnoise Monastery
21. Trim Castle
22. Adare Castle

Shetland Islands

Inverness

Aberdeen

EDINBURGH

Glasgow

17

Newcastle upon tyne

Londonderry **19**

Donegal

NORTHERN IRELAND

BELFAST

18

13

York

14

Liverpool

Manchester

21

Galway

DUBLIN

15

Caernarfon

12

IRELAND

20

22

Limerick

Waterford

ENGLAND

Norwich

Killarney

Birmingham

11

10

Cambridge

WALES

16

Oxford

7

CARDIFF

2

9

LONDON

8

Bristol

3

6

4

5

Dover

Southampton

Brighton

Exeter

1

0 10 20 30 40 50 60 miles
0 10 20 40 60 80 100 km

124

CERNE ABBAS GIANT

SITE LOCATION: CERNE ABBAS, DORSET See map p.123 (1)
CONSTRUCTION DATE: c.1000BC–AD1694
SPECIAL FEATURES: BEAUTIFUL LOCATION

The age of the extraordinary, club-wielding, sexually aroused giant carved into the hills above the village of Cerne Abbas in Dorset is a matter of some debate.

The first written reference to the giant comes as late as 1694, which, given that there is a huge archive of local documents about the area, implies that the giant may not have been there in medieval times. Either it was a later creation or it was discovered relatively recently and its outline then rechalked.

A record from 1774, written by a local vicar, the Reverend John Hutchins, refers to the giant as a recent creation: he says that it was cut into the hillside by Lord Holles, who owned the hill between 1642 and 1666 and detested Oliver Cromwell, the Lord Protector, whom the giant may well satirize.

Similar accusations of modernity were made about the Uffington White Horse, but recent scientific advances suggest that the horse, at least, may be 3,000 years old. Tests may eventually reveal the giant to be equally ancient. Whatever his true age, the Cerne Abbas Giant is certainly a fascinating and much-loved archaeological curiosity.

High on its hill, the Cerne Abbas Giant dominates the surrounding landscape. ▶

(i) information

Contact details

Cerne Abbas Giant
Cerne Abbas
Dorchester, Dorset

☎ +44 (0)1297 561900

 National Trust site
www.nationaltrust.org.uk
/main/w-chl/w-countryside
_environment/w-archaeology
/w-archaeology-places_to_visit
/w-archaeology-
cerne_abbas_giant.htm

Transport links

🚗 13 km (8 miles) north
of Dorchester on the A352

LACOCK ABBEY

SITE LOCATION: NEAR CHIPPENHAM, WILTSHIRE   See map p.123 ②
CONSTRUCTION DATE: 13TH CENTURY
SPECIAL FEATURES: A MIXTURE OF ARCHITECTURAL STYLES

Founded in 1229 by Ela, Countess of Salisbury for a group of Augustinian nuns, Lacock Abbey was dissolved in 1539 by Henry VIII (r. 1509–47). Eleven years later, the abbey, cloisters, chapter house and sacristy were incorporated into a new country house and thus saved for future generations. As a result, Lacock is a unique combination of architectural styles.

Remarkably, only one family – the Talbots – occupied the house from 1550 until it was given to the National Trust in the mid-20th century. Sir William Sharrington had converted the abbey

▼ *Lacock Abbey in Wiltshire still includes some of the original 13th-century Augustinian abbey.*

in 1550, but when he died childless in 1553 the abbey passed to his niece, Mrs John Talbot. The Talbots remained at Lacock until 1944. In the intervening centuries some changes were made to the house – it was given a superficial Gothic makeover in the 1750s and more work was carried out in the 1820s – but these were not hugely damaging to the original fabric of the house.

Lacock's greatest claim to fame is William Henry Fox Talbot, the pioneering photographer, who lived here. His earliest picture, taken in 1835, was of an oriel window at the abbey. There is a museum of photography in the abbey's gatehouse that celebrates his work.

The abbey's woodland garden is Victorian in style, but an elaborate

 A medieval barn, still standing in nearby Lacock village, is open to the public.

18th-century water garden is almost certainly hidden beneath it, awaiting the attentions of future archaeologists.

(i) information

Contact details

Lacock
Near Chippenham
Wiltshire
SN15 2LG

☎ +44 (0)1249 730459

🖳 National Trust site
www.nationaltrust.org.uk
/main/w-vh/w-visits
/w-findaplace
/w-lacockabbeyvillage

Transport links

🚗 Exit the M4 at junction 17, taking the A350 south via Chippenham. Lacock Abbey is about 5 km (3 miles) south of Chippenham

🚌 Chippenham–Frome services X34 and 234

🚆 Melksham 5 km (3 miles); Chippenham 5.6 km (3½ miles)

MALMESBURY ABBEY

SITE LOCATION: MALMESBURY, WILTSHIRE   See map p.123

CONSTRUCTION DATE: 12TH CENTURY

SPECIAL FEATURES: SUPERB VAULTED ROOF ABOVE THE NAVE

The mostly 12th-century remains of this once-remote abbey in Wiltshire represent only about one-third of the original buildings. However, given the amount of destruction caused by the Dissolution of the Monasteries in 1536 it is remarkable that so much of it survives to this day.

Malmesbury is often said to be the place where the Cotswolds meet the West Country, which may have been the reason why a monastery was established there in *c*.676 by Aldhelm. The location's importance can also be judged by the fact that Athelstan (r. *c*.924–39), the first king of a united England, is buried here.

The present abbey was built in the 12th century and consecrated in *c*.1180. The mid-12th-century south porch, through which visitors enter today, is a splendid piece of Norman work and there is a superb vaulted roof above the nave. The church originally had a spire taller than that at Salisbury Cathedral but it collapsed in the 16th century.

After the Dissolution, a local man – William Stump – bought the site and converted it into the parish church.

 Much of 12th-century Malmesbury Abbey remains intact despite damage caused by the Dissolution.

ⓘ information

Contact details

Malmesbury Abbey
The Abbey Office
Holloway
Malmesbury
SN16 9BA

☎ +44 (0)1666 826 666

 Malmesbury Abbey
www.malmesburyabbey.info

Transport links

 From the M4, exit at junction 17 onto the A429 to Malmesbury, which is about 8 km (5 miles) away

ST BOTOLPH'S, HARDHAM

130

SITE LOCATION: HARDHAM, WEST SUSSEX   See map p.123 ④

CONSTRUCTION DATE: POST-1066

SPECIAL FEATURES: MEDIEVAL WALL PAINTINGS

Almost every aspect of church-going today would be unfamiliar to our medieval ancestors. If you want to see with your own eyes what pretty much every parish church in the country would have looked like before Henry VIII (r. 1509–47) fell out with the pope you must visit this tiny, little-known church in Hardham, West Sussex.

▼ *St Botolph's is a prime example of a parish church from the late Middle Ages.*

St Botolph's is largely Norman; it is very small because more than 900 years ago this was a remote and very poor rural community. The importance of the church in out-of-the-way places like this, however, can be judged by St Botolph's wall paintings, which have given archaeologists and historians some remarkable insights into religious life in a small rural community in the late Middle Ages.

Other churches have more spectacular individual wall paintings but none has retained almost all of its original work in the way that St Botolph's has. Virtually every surface – from the sides of the nave to the chancel arch and the altar – is covered with beautifully executed scenes from the life of Christ, as well as extraordinary pictures of Adam and Eve, including one showing Eve milking a cow; another picture shows the serenity of heaven and the horrors of hell. The apostles are also portrayed, as well as St George slaying the dragon.

The point to remember about these extraordinary works of art is that they were painted to instruct a largely illiterate

▲ *The extensive medieval paintings at St Botolph's would have helped instruct an illiterate congregation.*

population and it is believed that the images in St Botolph's were the work of a group of painters working about 1100 and specifically employed to travel the country painting such scenes. Before the Reformation, beginning in 1529, most churches in England would have contained comparable scenes. It is ironic that the whitewash that eventually covered the pictures helped preserve them for us today.

(i) information

Contact details

St Botolph's
Hardham
West Sussex
RH20 1LB

☎ +44 (0)1798 839057

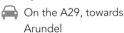 **Church of England site**
www.achurchnearyou.com
/hardham-st-botolph

Transport links

 On the A29, towards Arundel

 Pulborough, 2 km (1⅛ miles)

WINCHELSEA

SITE LOCATION: NEAR RYE, EAST SUSSEX

CONSTRUCTION DATE: *c.*13TH CENTURY

SPECIAL FEATURES: MEDIEVAL WINE CELLARS

See map p.123 **5**

The quiet village of Winchelsea on the East Sussex coast was once one of the busiest ports in England. Over 700 years ago, it was part of the vitally important Confederation of Cinque Ports, charged with providing ships and men to defend the kingdom in times of war before the Royal Navy came into existence in the 16th century.

The evidence for Winchelsea's former commercial importance still exists beneath the streets, where, untouched for centuries, is a mass of medieval wine cellars. In medieval and later times, ships from Winchelsea traded with the world, sailing across the North Sea and as far south as the Bay of Biscay, off western France and northern Spain.

Still visible in the town are remnants of its once-huge medieval church of St Thomas the Martyr, as well as three magnificent medieval gates. It also retains its medieval street pattern with little later alteration.

Winchelsea was built in 1281 at the instigation of Edward I (r. 1272–1307) to replace an earlier town of the same name, which was destroyed by the sea in the 1200s. It was built from scratch to a fixed plan, perched on a hilltop. By 1600, the town had lost its importance as a port when the River Brede estuary silted up. The fact that it did not develop into a big modern town is precisely the reason why it now preserves so many features of medieval life for us to see today.

The present church in Winchelsea is a remnant of the once-huge medieval church of St Thomas the Martyr.

(i) information

Contact details

Winchelsea
East Sussex

 The Ancient Town
of Winchelsea

www.winchelsea.net

Transport links

 Off the A259, 13 km
(8 miles) east of Hastings;
5 km (3 miles) west of Rye

 Winchelsea

134

DOVER CASTLE

SITE LOCATION:	DOVER, KENT
CONSTRUCTION DATE:	POST-1066
SPECIAL FEATURES:	MASSIVE KEEP AND ROMAN LIGHTHOUSE

See map p.123 ⑥

Dover Castle, strategically located at the point of the shortest crossing from England to mainland Europe, is one of southern England's most remarkable and well-preserved medieval fortresses.

An Anglo–Saxon fortress, including a Roman lighthouse, existed on the site when the Normans conquered England in 1066. Soon after, the Normans strengthened the fortress and built a castle. Not much remains of this castle, but it was probably centred on the Roman lighthouse – which still exists – and the Anglo–Saxon church. In the 1180s, a little over a century after the Norman Conquest, Henry II (r. 1154–89) commissioned Maurice the Engineer to rebuild the castle, adding a massive keep within several lines of defence.

The castle stood successfully against a siege (1216–17), when Prince Louis of

▼ *Dover Castle dominates the narrowest crossing to the mainland of Europe.*

France invaded south-east England and tried to overthrow King John (r. 1199–1216).

By the time Henry VIII (r. 1509–47) split from Rome in 1533, the castle was a vital bulwark against possible invasion by forces from Catholic mainland Europe, especially after 1538 when France entered a truce with Spain. The threat led to the strengthening of the castle, which appears to have been supervised by the king himself.

In the 18th century, accommodation for extra troops was built within the castle walls and the interiors of the castle keep and other buildings were modernized during the Napoleonic Wars (1803–15) and again during the latter part of the 19th century. Beneath the chalk cliffs around Dover is a beautifully constructed maze of underground tunnels built during the Napoleonic Wars.

Another fascinating relic of the Napoleonic era is the triple staircase known as the Grand Shaft: three clockwise staircases that rise up, one above the other, from Dover's Snargate Street through a shaft 8 metres (26 feet) in diameter cut through the cliffs to the Western Heights – the cliff-top defences built to protect England against invasion during the Napoleonic Wars. Hidden from view, the Grand Shaft was built to allow troops to get from the town to their defensive positions as quickly as possible. Before it was built, the soldiers had to clamber down steep chalky trackways that were treacherous during bad weather.

During the Second World War (1939–45), a hospital was built at the castle, as well as a command centre for the evacuation of Dunkirk. The army left in 1958. Today, the castle is owned by English Heritage.

(i) information

Contact details

Dover Castle
Harold's Road
Dover
Kent CT16 1HU

☎ +44 (0)1304 211067

 English Heritage site

www.english-heritage.org.uk
/daysout/properties
/dover-castle

Transport links

 On east side of Dover, signposted from the M20, A2 (junction 1 of the M2) and the town centre

 Service 15/X in East Kent; service 593 from Dover

 Dover Priory, 2.4 km (1½ miles)

CRESSING TEMPLE BARNS

SITE LOCATION: CRESSING TEMPLE, ESSEX   See map p.123 (7)
CONSTRUCTION DATE: *c.*13TH CENTURY
SPECIAL FEATURES: INTRICATE TIMBERWORK

Cressing Temple Barns are perhaps the greatest of England's archetypal 'cathedral' barns. There are actually two barns at the Cressing Temple estate in Essex. The earlier of the barns, known as the Barley Barn, was originally built in 1137 (and rebuilt *c.*1200) at the instigation of the monastic, military

▼ *The cathedral-like dimensions of the Wheat Barn are a spectacular sight.*

Order of the Knights Templar. The later barn, known as the Wheat Barn, was built in *c.*1280 and has been likened to a cathedral, with its mass of intricate timberwork, vast interior and aisled pillars.

The role of the Knights Templar was to protect pilgrims on their journeys to the Holy Land. The land in Essex, where they built their barn, had been given to them by Queen Matilda, wife of King Stephen (r. 1135–54). Here, they established farms and used the profits generated by their produce to fund their activities.

The estate also has 16th-century stables and a granary, which along with the barns, give a remarkable archaeological glimpse into a long-vanished farming traditions going back many centuries.

Archaeological evidence – particularly pottery and flintwork – from the site indicates that this corner of Essex has been inhabited by humans since 1500BC in the Bronze Age, and there was certainly an Iron Age (*c.*700BC–AD43) settlement here, too.

In 1312, the Order of the Knights Templar was disbanded by Pope Clement V

▲ *Built originally for the Knights Templar, the Barley Barn is a superb example of medieval engineering.*

and Cressing Temple passed to the Knights Hospitallers, another monastic order established with the aim of caring for the needs of pilgrims intent on journeying to the Holy Land.

The farm suffered damage during the Peasants' Revolt of 1381. This event may be reflected in clear evidence that the barns were extensively repaired and even remodelled in the late 14th century.

By 1540, the Knights Hospitallers had also been suppressed by papal decree and the first in a long line of secular owners began their stewardship of this remarkable site.

Today, visitors to the estate can see – in addition to the barns, stables and granary – a walled Tudor garden, containing plants cultivated during that period, and a 17th-century farmhouse.

ⓘ information

Contact details

Cressing Temple
Witham Road
Cressing
Braintree
CM77 8PD

☎ +44 (0)1376 584903

🖥 **Country Parks site**
www.visitparks.co.uk/placest
ovisit/cressingtemple.php

Transport links

 Located on the B1080 (Braintree–Witham road)

 Witham

TOWER OF LONDON

SITE LOCATION: TOWER HILL, LONDON
CONSTRUCTION DATE: POST-1066
SPECIAL FEATURES: EARLY GRAFITTI AND CROWN JEWELS

See map p.123 ⑧

Construction of the Tower of London began soon after the Norman victory of 1066, as part of the great programme of castle-building that followed the conquest.

Virtually every royal monarch since William the Conqueror (r. 1066–87) has added something to the Tower of London. The famous White Tower, the oldest remaining structure on the site, was the centre of a complex designed as a place where the royal family could consolidate their power and a retreat in times of trouble. By 1190, work had begun to encircle the White Tower with two walls and a moat.

Henry III (r. 1216–72) extended the royal accommodation and built two towers on the waterfront, the Wakefield Tower and the Lanthorn Tower (the latter was rebuilt in the 19th century). Henry also built a new curtain wall around the east, west and north sides of the castle, thereby enclosing the church of St Peter ad Vincula.

Edward I (r. 1272–1307) built the Beauchamp Tower, destroyed Henry III's moat and built a new curtain wall and moat as well as royal lodgings in St Thomas's Tower. Edward III (r. 1327–77) began the next major works by building a wharf which was not completed until the time of Richard II (r. 1377–99).

Throughout its history, the castle has housed many famous prisoners, such as Edward V (r. 1483) and his brother Richard ('The Princes in the Tower'), Lady Jane Grey ('The Nine Days' Queen' of 1553), the future Elizabeth I (r. 1558–1603) and, in more recent times, prominent Nazi Rudolf Hess, who was held in the Tower during the Second World War (1939–45).

During the 17th and 18th centuries, medieval lodgings were destroyed and more military buildings added. Of these, only the New Armouries survive today.

The Victorian architect Anthony Salvin remodelled parts of the castle to restore its medieval look, but his idea of medieval was wildly fanciful – part of a general craze at the time for highly unhistoric recreations of the past. In 1843, the moat was drained. Amazingly, although some later buildings were hit during the Second World War, the White Tower remained entirely unscathed.

▲ *The Tower of London has dominated the city for nearly 1,000 years.*

ⓘ information

Contact details

The Tower of London
City of London
EC3N 4AB

☎ 0844 482 7777 (UK)
+44 (0)20 3166 6000
(outside the UK)

🖥 **Historic Royal Palaces site**
www.hrp.org.uk
/toweroflondon

Transport links

⊖ Tower Hill or DLR Tower
Gateway

🚆 Fenchurch Street or
London Bridge

🚌 Services 15, 42, 78 and 100

🚢 Tower Pier

ST OSWALD'S, WIDFORD

SITE LOCATION: OXFORDSHIRE   See map p.123 (9)
CONSTRUCTION DATE: c.12TH CENTURY
SPECIAL FEATURES: 18TH CENTURY PEWS AND ROMAN MOSAIC

The best way to approach St Oswald's Church, Widford, is through the beautiful Cotswold town of Burford, its ancient golden stone houses climbing the hillside. Half-way down Burford's steep hill, a narrow right turn is signposted to the villages of Swinford and Widford.

Swinford is best known as the childhood home of the controversial, aristocratic Mitford sisters, but well before Swinford the sharp-eyed visitor may spot in an apparently empty field to the left and on a slope above the River Windrush a small rather lonely looking church. In fact, the church is so tiny it is really only a chapel. This is St Oswald's Church. The single-celled chapel has many ghostly traces of its original wall paintings and is the last remnant of an abandoned medieval village.

Traces of the lanes and houses that stood here before the Black Death devastated the village in the Middle Ages can be clearly seen in the odd lumps and bumps across the field surrounding the chapel.

Most fascinating of all, there is a Roman mosaic beneath the church. The old church flagstones are sometimes lifted so visitors can see traces of the mosaic, thought to have been part of a Roman villa.

St Oswald's Church is still occasionally used for services and it still has its 18th-century wooden box pews.

 The tiny church of St Oswald's, Widford, still has its 18th-century box pews.

(i) information

Contact details

St Oswald's, Widford
Near Burford
Oxfordshire
OX18 4DX

 Oxfordshire Cotswolds
www.oxfordshirecotswolds.org
/site/attractions/widford-st-
oswald-s-church-p457601

Transport links

 Off the A40, 29 km
(18 miles) from Oxford

KENILWORTH CASTLE

SITE LOCATION: KENILWORTH, WARWICKSHIRE   See map p.123 (10)
CONSTRUCTION DATE: *c.*11TH CENTURY
SPECIAL FEATURES: TUDOR GARDENS

Kenilworth Castle is the largest castle ruin in England. Building began about 50 years after the Norman Conquest of 1066 and by 1166 Henry II (r. 1154–89) was able to use the castle as a base from which to attack his own son's rebellious army. King John (r. 1199–1216) extended the castle and its lake and in 1253 Henry III (r. 1216–72) gave it to powerful baron Simon de Montfort. It was back in royal hands in the early 15th century and Henry V (r. 1413–22) built a banqueting house here.

In the 16th century, the castle passed to the Dudley family, the most famous of whom, John, Duke of Northumberland, was executed after placing his daughter-in-law

▼ *The inner castle is protected by a magnificent curtain wall that retains its towers.*

▲ *The new red sandstone used to build Kenilworth Castle was quarried locally.*

Lady Jane Grey on the throne in 1553. Reclaimed by the crown, the castle was later returned to John's son, Robert, a favourite of Elizabeth I (r. 1558–1603). The castle was extended and improved for the queen's visits. In 1575, Elizabeth spent 19 days here, lavishly entertained with fireworks, music and dancing.

Damaged during the English Civil War (1642–51), the castle fell into disrepair and over the next few centuries it became the ruin that we see today.

ⓘ information

Contact details

Kenilworth Castle
Kenilworth
Warwickshire
CV8 1NE

 +44 (0)1926 852078

 English Heritage site

www.english-heritage.org.uk
/daysout/properties
/kenilworth-castle/

Transport links

🚗 In Kenilworth, off the A46. Clearly signposted from the town centre

 Coventry and Leamington Spa, 8 km (5 miles); Warwick, 11.3 km (7 miles)

STOKESAY CASTLE

SITE LOCATION: **STOKESAY, SHROPSHIRE** See map p.123 **11**
CONSTRUCTION DATE: **13TH CENTURY**
SPECIAL FEATURES: **TIMBER GATEHOUSE**

Lawrence Ludlow, a wool merchant, built his manor house at Stokesay in Shropshire towards the end of the 13th century – it has been called a castle only since the 16th century – and it has remained virtually unaltered for almost 700 years.

Ludlow built his manor house with some fortifications, even though he knew he was building at a time when the Welsh borders were at peace, following the defeat of Prince Llywelyn of Wales by English king Edward I (r. 1272–1307).

The house originally had an artificial moat, fed by a lake to the south-west. The north and south towers of the castle are divided by the great hall. Although part of the curtain wall between the south tower and the hall was rebuilt in the 17th century, the rest of the building – except the beautiful Elizabethan timber-framed gatehouse from the 16th century – stands today almost exactly as it did in Ludlow's time.

After the Ludlows, a series of families owned Stokesay Castle. By the 19th century, it was being used as farm buildings and fell into disrepair. Since 1850, however, the castle has been preserved and in 1992 it was given to English Heritage.

◀ *The fortified manor house at Stokesay dates back to the 13th century.*

ⓘ information

Contact details

Stokesay Castle
Near Craven Arms
Shropshire
SY7 9AH

☎ +44 (0)1588 672544

 English Heritage site
www.english-heritage.org.uk
/daysout/properties
/stokesay-castle

Transport links

 11.3 km (7 miles) north-west of Ludlow, off the A49

 Craven Arms, 1.6 km (1 mile)

LITTLE MORETON HALL

SITE LOCATION: CONGLETON, CHESHIRE   See map p.123 (11)

CONSTRUCTION DATE: 15TH CENTURY

SPECIAL FEATURES: LEADED WINDOWS

Little Moreton Hall in Cheshire is one of the best-preserved and least-altered Tudor houses in Britain and is a remarkably rare example of a timber-framed house from that time.

The house was built over three generations and a period of about 130 years. It was owned by the Moreton family from the time it was completed in the mid-1400s until it was given to the National Trust by a member of the family in the late 1930s – an extraordinary record of ownership by any standards.

The eastern portion of the house has the earliest surviving architecture, the east wing and great hall being pretty much exactly today as they were when first completed in the mid-15th century. In the 1550s, carpenter Richard Dale was commissioned to modernize some parts of the old house and remodel others.

The windows in Little Moreton Hall are particularly remarkable. The leaded glass is mostly 16th century, and its fine, delicate quality reveals a wonderful range of colours even today.

Over the centuries, the hall has been added to and has become a curious mix of architectural styles, formed around a courtyard. There isn't a single straight line anywhere and the roof timbers and heavy slates have caused the walls to bow. None of this movement, however, in any way threatens the basic strength of the building. The advantage of early timber-framed buildings, compared to those made of brick or stone, is that they can move and shift – sometimes a great deal – without losing their fundamental strength. For archaeologists, therefore, Moreton Hall is a mine of information about early building techniques.

At the end of the 19th century, the enlightened Elizabeth Moreton decided to restore the house sympathetically without major reworking. Her renovations were continued by her cousin and heir, Bishop Charles Abraham. In 1938, wishing to secure the future of such an outstanding example of period architecture, Bishop Abraham presented the house to the National Trust, who now maintains it.

▲ The south wing of the moated Little Moreton Hall was added to the house in c.1570.

(i) information

Contact details

Little Moreton Hall
Congleton
Cheshire
CW12 4SD

☎ +44 (0)1260 272018

 National Trust site

www.nationaltrust.org.uk
/main/w-littlemoretonhall

Transport links

 6.5 km (4 miles) south-west of Congleton, off the A34

 Alsager–Congleton service 315

 Kidsgrove, 5 km (3 miles); Congleton, 7.2 km (4½ miles)

148

RIEVAULX ABBEY

SITE LOCATION: NEAR HELMSLEY, NORTH YORKSHIRE   See map p.123 **(12)**

CONSTRUCTION DATE: *c.*12TH CENTURY

SPECIAL FEATURES: BEAUTIFUL LOCATION

Rievaulx Abbey in North Yorkshire has a ghostly, haunted air. Founded in 1131, it was once home to more than 150 monks and an astonishing 500 lay brethren. Much of the church attached to Rievaulx survives intact, but despite the extensive remains over the rest of the site what we see today is less than half of what once stood here.

The original buildings were austere and plain in style, being based closely on the mother house at Clairvaux in France. Some time after Rievaulx was built, part of the eastern end was demolished, and the buildings erected to replace those taken down were characterized by far more elegant and decorative work.

The beautiful dining hall, which is more than 37 metres (124 feet) long, is one of the best-preserved parts of the abbey. An undercroft skilfully built into the terraced banks of the river supports the imposing 15-metre (50-feet) high walls with their elegant arched lancet windows and beautiful arcading.

In 1538, during the Dissolution of the Monasteries, Rievaulx was stripped of its treasures and allowed to fall into decay. It is now looked after by English Heritage.

This majestic view of the abbey ruins inspired Turner and other Romantic artists in the 1820s. ▶

(i) information

Contact details

Rievaulx Abbey
Near Helmsley
North Yorkshire
YO62 5LB

☎ +44 (0)1439 798228

 English Heritage site
www.english-heritage.org.uk
/daysout/properties
/rievaulx-abbey/

Transport links

 3.6 km (2¼ miles) north of Helmsley, off the B1257

 Services M8, M91 and H2 from Helmsley

150

FURNESS ABBEY

SITE LOCATION: NEAR BARROW-IN-FURNESS, CUMBRIA   See map p.123 **(13)**
CONSTRUCTION DATE: 12TH CENTURY
SPECIAL FEATURES: ATMOSPHERIC RUINS

Furness Abbey in Cumbria was established in 1127 by Stephen of Blois (later King Stephen; r. 1135–54) and built for Savigniac monks from the north of France. It is a classic example of a monastery that is deliberately sited in as remote a position as possible. When the abbey was founded, its isolation, between the Lake District and Morecambe Bay, must have seemed as if it was at the end of the earth.

The abbey became a self-sufficient Cistercian foundation in 1147, as enthusiasm

▼ *The impressive ruins of Furness Abbey came to symbolize the Romantic era's love of the Gothic through works such as Wordsworth's 'The Prelude'.*

for the Cistercian way of life swept across Europe. The abbey became immensely rich, gaining much of its wealth from trade in wool. The buildings were extended over the ensuing centuries and completely remodelled in the 15th century before the destruction that met every monastic foundation during the Dissolution of the Monasteries in 1537.

Furness was seen as a particularly romantic ruin as early as the end of the 18th century. Other monastic ruins – including Fountains Abbey in North Yorkshire – began to be preserved at this time as a new enthusiasm for the medieval developed. English Romantic poet William Wordsworth wrote about Furness in his great autobiographical poem 'The Prelude' (1805); Furness was also painted by Turner and came to symbolize the late 18th and early 19th centuries' great love of the romantic gothic ruin.

The substantial ruins we see today are beautifully set in the wooded Beckansgill Valley. They are largely constructed of red sandstone and the surviving elements are impressive – the arched entrance to the cloister is a superb example of Norman work, for example. A museum contains many of the fine stone carvings that have been recovered from the site.

Visitors can still see impressive remains of the church where the monks would have spent much of the day and night at their devotions, as well as the chapter house and cloister and the more practical parts of the building: the lavatorium, refectory and kitchens. You can even still see the skilled engineering of the drainage system that channelled large amounts of water into the kitchen and out of the lavatories. Emergency restoration work is presently being carried out to prevent the collapse of sections of the abbey.

ⓘ information

Contact details

Furness Abbey
Manor Road
Near Barrow-in-Furness
Cumbria
LA13 0PJ

☎ +44 (0)1229 823420

🖳 **English Heritage site**
www.english-heritage.org.uk
/daysout/properties
/furness-abbey/

Transport links

 2.4 km (1½ miles) north of Barrow-in-Furness

 Barrow-in-Furness–Ulverston service 6/A, to within 1.2 km (¾ mile) of the ruins

 Barrow-in-Furness, 3.2 km (2 miles)

CONWY CASTLE

SITE LOCATION: CONWY, WALES See map p.123 (14)
CONSTRUCTION DATE: 13TH CENTURY
SPECIAL FEATURES: TOWN WALL AND TOWERS

Conwy Castle in Wales was built between 1283 and 1289 for the king of England Edward I (r. 1272–1307). It was more of a fortified town than a conventional castle, with almost 1,280 metres (1,400 yards) of wall, 7 metres (24 feet) thick and 9 metres (30 feet) high, much of which can still be walked today. The wall has 21 towers, 3 gateways and encloses Conwy town.

Designated a UNESCO World Heritage Site in 1986, Conwy is remarkably well preserved and reveals in great detail the enormous skill of the medieval military engineers who were commissioned to build a castle that would be a statement of English dominance, sufficient to awe the local population into submission.

Siege was the greatest threat to medieval castles, which is why so many, Conwy among them, were built on the coast or an estuary so that they could be supplied by ship. Within its thick walls, Edward's eight-storey castle was surrounded on three sides by water. On the town side, the castle's outer ward housed the garrison. In the inner ward, the king's private apartments were built,

still crowned by its original turrets. These apartments were protected by both the town wall and the outer ward, two strong lines of defence that, it would have been assumed, could never be breached.

The key to the defence of the castle is the fact that every length of wall can be defended from a number of angles, so that there would be nowhere for an attacking force to escape the counter-attack of the castle's defenders: the towers overlook each other and the walls below them.

However, no castle is impregnable to a sustained and sufficiently skilful attack. Eventually Conwy fell, captured in 1401 by the great hero and Prince of Wales Owain Glyndwr (r. 1400–16). Conwy Castle was subsequently retaken by Lord Herbert during the Wars of the Roses (1455–85) and in 1685 it was granted to the Earl of Conwy.

The local authority took over the site in the 19th century, thereby saving it from damage or even destruction, and the castle is now looked after by the government body Cadw (Welsh Historic Monuments).

▲ *Conwy is far more than a fortified castle – it is part of a fortified town, with 10-metre (30-feet) thick walls.*

(i) information

Contact details

Conwy Castle
Rose Hill Street
Conwy, Gwynedd
LL32 8LD

☎ +44 (0)1492 592358

 **Conwy Castle and Town**
www.conwy.com

Transport links

🚗 Conwy is on the A55 and B5106

🚆 Conwy station is next to the castle

ST DAVID'S CATHEDRAL

SITE LOCATION: PEMBROKESHIRE, WALES   See map p.123

CONSTRUCTION DATE: 12TH CENTURY

SPECIAL FEATURES: BISHOP'S PALACE

On the edge of the far north-west coast of Pembrokeshire, past a series of little bays, slate quarries and long-abandoned quarry tramways, the visitor reaches St David's Head, where the remains of prehistoric fields and an Iron Age fort can still be seen. A few kilometres south from here is the smallest cathedral city in Britain: St David's.

The first monastery here was established in the 6th century by the patron saint of Wales, David, who was the son of a Welsh prince. This remote location provided the monks with ideal surroundings in which to contemplate God. The monastery also had the great advantage of looking out towards that most holy place – Ireland.

But, like so many early monasteries, St David's was attacked by Vikings throughout the following centuries, and during these attacks the original 6th-century buildings were destroyed. The red sandstone building that we see today dates from the 12th century and has one particularly striking feature: its floor slopes upwards towards the altar. The ruins of the bishop's palace, with its magnificent round window in the Great Hall, can also be seen.

 St David's is the most ancient cathedral settlement in the British Isles.

(i) information

Contact details

The Deanery Office
St David's Cathedral
The Close, St David's
Pembrokeshire
SA62 6RH

 +44 (0)1437 720202

 St David's Cathedral
www.stdavidscathedral.org.uk

Transport links

Off the A487 at St David's

Haverfordwest, 26 km (16 miles)

MELROSE ABBEY

SITE LOCATION: NEAR GALASHIELS, SCOTLAND See map p.123 (16)
CONSTRUCTION DATE: c.12TH–16TH CENTURY
SPECIAL FEATURES: ON-SITE MUSEUM

In the 7th century, the Irish monk St Aidan, having founded a monastery at Lindisfarne in the far north-east of England, set off for Scotland and promptly founded another monastery. Situated on land within a dramatic loop in the River Tweed, the monastery – which housed monks from Iona – was destroyed by Scottish king Kenneth McAlpin (r. 843–58) during raids in 839.

Several centuries later, in 1136, Scottish king David I (r. 1124–53) invited a group of Cistercian monks from Rievaulx Abbey in North Yorkshire to build a new abbey where St Aidan's monastery had once been. The new monks wanted good farmland so they chose what is now Melrose, instead, 3 kilometres (2 miles) from St Aidan's site.

The first part of the church to be built was the east end. We know that it was dedicated in June 1146, but it took a further 50 years before the monastery was more or less complete.

In 1322, disaster struck when the abbey and the town that had grown up around it were destroyed by the English army of Edward II (r. 1307–27). Rebuilding of the abbey began almost immediately and Scottish king Robert the Bruce (r. 1306–29) helped fund the work – which is why his heart, encased in a lead box, is said to be buried here. After the Scottish invasion of England in 1385, however, the army of the English king Richard II (r. 1377–99) pushed the Scots back and destroyed the abbey again.

Undaunted by the disasters of the past, the monks began to rebuild again. This time, the work was not completed until a century later. In fact, parts of the church were still being built in the early 1500s and it may be that the west end of the abbey church was never completed as planned.

In 1544, the army of English king Henry VIII (r. 1509–47) invaded Scotland to try to persuade the Scots to agree to a marriage between Henry's son Edward and the infant Mary, Queen of Scots (r. 1542–67). Melrose was badly damaged again. Ironically, it was not suppressed during the Dissolution of the Monasteries. In 1560, the monks accepted the Scottish Reformation, but they were saddled with a decaying building and

 Melrose is unusual in that a very large amount of it remains, including the Commendator's House, which is now used as a museum. Melrose is also the place where Robert the Bruce's heart is said to be buried.

no funds to repair it. The last monk died at the abbey in 1590 and it was abandoned until 1610, when the nave of the abbey church was converted into a church. This remained Melrose's parish church until 1810.

Melrose is a particularly interesting site because so much remains of the abbey church, along with the foundations of the other buildings that made up the original complex. The Commendator's House, which dates back to the 1400s (the commendator was a titular abbot, who benefited from the income attached to the post) is now a museum.

(i) information

Contact details

Melrose Abbey
Melrose
Scottish Borders
TD6 9LG

 +44 (0)1896 822 562

 Historic Scotland site
www.historic-scotland.
gov.uk/propertyresults
/propertyoverview.htm?
PropID=PL_210&PropName
=MelroseAbbey

Transport links

In Melrose, near Galashiels, off the A7 or A68

158

CAERLAVEROCK CASTLE

SITE LOCATION: CAERLAVEROCK, SCOTLAND   see map p.123 **17**
CONSTRUCTION DATE: 13TH CENTURY
SPECIAL FEATURES: SPECTACULAR LOCATION

Caerlaverock Castle, built to control the south-west approaches to Scotland across the Solway Firth, is situated in one of the most spectacular spots imaginable. Despite its great age, this is not the only castle to have been erected here – the present building dates back to the 13th century, but a slightly older castle existed near the

▼ *Caerlaverock Castle in Scotland is surrounded and protected by a deep moat.*

same site. The first castle was built some 180 metres (200 yards) from the present building in an area of marshland, and the damp, unwholesome nature of the setting may well be the reason why this original castle was abandoned just 50 years or so after it was built.

Only a grassy mound is left of that first, abandoned castle, but the site has proved a great draw for archaeologists, and recent digs have uncovered evidence of a curtain wall and a tower. Among the many finds have been some precisely datable items: for example, a coin discovered during excavations is a halfpenny from the reign of the Scottish king William the Lion (r. 1165–1214), which was probably lost some time between 1210 and 1250.

The new castle had a chequered history. In 1300, it was besieged by the English king Edward I (1272–1307) during his war against the Scottish king John Balliol (r. 1292–96). Scottish king Robert the Bruce (r. 1306–29) damaged it so badly that it was uninhabitable until the 15th century, when it was rebuilt. The reconstruction adhered closely to the design of the original castle, but the gatehouse was strengthened and comfortable living rooms, including a three-storey set of apartments built up against the inner eastern wall, were added by the 1st Earl of Nithsdale. These were probably completed in the 1630s; their remains survive today. Caerlaverock is a fascinating site and is unique in that it was built to a triangular plan, with a tower at each corner and a double moat.

A written record survives of an episode during the castle's early days. A French knight wrote an account of the siege of 1300. He tells us in plain terms that 'Caerlaverock was so strong a castle that it feared no siege.'

ⓘ information

Contact details

Caerlaverock Castle
Glencaple House
Church Street
Glencaple
Dumfries
DG1 4RU

☎ +44 (0)1387 770 244

 Historic Scotland site
www.historic-scotland.
gov.uk/propertyresults
/propertyplan.htm?PropID
=PL_047&PropName=
CaerlaverockCastle

Transport links

 13 km (8 miles) south-east
of Dumfries on the B725

 Dumfries, 9 km (5½ miles)

 Dumfries–Caerlaverock
service D6A

DUNLUCE

SITE LOCATION: NEAR BUSHMILLS, NORTHERN IRELAND   See map p.123 (**19**)
CONSTRUCTION DATE: 13TH–16TH CENTURY
SPECIAL FEATURES: SPECTACULAR POSITION

Along Ireland's wild northern coast are the remains of a series of impressive castles and among the greatest of these is Dunluce.

There has probably been a fortified stronghold of some kind on this rocky promontory since the 11th century, if not earlier, but the castle ruin we see today is the product of two building periods. Richard Óg de Burgh, 2nd Earl of Ulster, is thought to have built the first castle in the 13th century. In the 1500s, the MacDonnells, who came to Ireland originally from the Hebrides, seized the castle and began rebuild to it.

The castle remained the principal residence of the MacDonnell family until the mid-17th century, after which Dunluce was allowed gradually to fall into disrepair for reasons that are not entirely clear.

Despite the skill of the builders who designed Dunluce to be impregnable, the power of the sea has at times been too much – in the mid-1600s a huge section of the castle's domestic quarters collapsed into the sea and a number of lives were lost.

Today the ruins can be reached by a wooden bridge that stretches precariously from the mainland to the castle entrance.

 In the 17th century, a huge section of Dunluce Castle collapsed into the sea.

(i) information

Contact details

Dunluce
87 Dunluce Road
Bushmills
County Antrim
BT57 8UY

 +44 (0)28 2073 1938

 Discover Northern Ireland site
www.discovernorthernireland.com
/Dunluce-Castle-Medieval-Irish-
Castle-on-the-Antrim-Coast-
Bushmills-P2819

Transport links

 On the A2 about 5 km
(3 miles) east of Portrush

CLONMACNOISE MONASTERY

SITE LOCATION: SHANNONBRIDGE, IRELAND See map p.123 **19**
CONSTRUCTION DATE: POST-1066
SPECIAL FEATURES: ROUND TOWERS AND EIGHT CHURCHES

Clonmacnoise Monastery in central Ireland is an extraordinary collection of ruins, including eight churches, a cathedral, two round towers, hundreds of cross slabs, a 13th-century castle and three high crosses. It was founded by St Ciarán in AD545.

In AD800, the monastery was sacked by the Vikings but subsequently rebuilt; when the Normans arrived after 1066, it was badly damaged again before being rebuilt once more and then finally made uninhabitable by English Parliamentary forces in the 17th century.

The great days for Clonmacnoise came under the patronage and protection of the High Kings of Ireland, including the last of the line, Rory O'Connor (r. 1166–98), who was buried here.

Recent excavations have revealed the true extent of the scale of Clonmacnoise. Indeed, the monastery was known as 'The City of Saints and Scholars', for it was a centre of study and learning at a time when mainland Britain was a dark place of warring, illiterate tribes.

The *Chronicon Scotorum*, a chronicle of Irish history up to 1135, was written here, as was the *Leabhar na hUidre* ('Book of the Dun Cow'), the oldest manuscript written in Irish still in existence.

Clonmacnoise is an extraordinary mix of churches, round towers, slabs and high crosses. ▶

ⓘ information

Contact details

Clonmacnoise Monastery
Shannonbridge
County Offaly
Republic of Ireland

 +353 (0)90 967 4195

 Heritage Ireland site
www.heritageireland.ie
/en/midlandseastcoast
/clonmacnoise

Transport links

 21 km (13 miles) from Athlone or 20 km (12½ miles) from Ballinasloe

164

TRIM CASTLE

SITE LOCATION: TRIM, COUNTY MEATH, IRELAND   See map p.123 **(20)**
CONSTRUCTION DATE: *c.*1176
SPECIAL FEATURES: 20-SIDED CRUCIFORM-SHAPED TOWER

Trim Castle on the banks of the River Boyne in County Meath was almost certainly the first castle in Ireland to be built of stone. The original fortification at Trim was most likely built in timber – soon replaced by stone – and was probably the work of the Anglo–Norman knight Hugh de Lacy in the late 12th century. In the second half of the 13th century, Geoffrey de Geneville carried out more work, remodelling the

▼ *Trim Castle – the biggest castle in Ireland – has a massive square keep and a round tower.*

moat, drawbridge and the North Tower, and building the Great Hall. The castle was badly damaged in 1649 during English Parliamentary leader Oliver Cromwell's suppression of the Royalists in Ireland.

Trim's dramatic square keep, with its four square towers, one on each wall (only three remain today), is more than 18 metres (60 feet) tall, with walls 3.5 metres (11 feet) thick. It was erected some way from the other buildings on a site that covers more than 1.2 hectares (3 acres).

The keep has three storeys and would originally have contained a great hall, a chapel and a small garrison, as well as rooms for a chaplain and various other officials. There was only one entrance to the keep, on the main floor of the east tower, below the chapel. In the south-west and north-east corners of the keep, there are winding staircases that link the three levels.

The vast outer curtain wall is 500 metres (546 yards) long, has eight towers and two gatehouses and forms a triangle around the keep. Two-thirds of it still survives.

Trim Gate, the main entrance, faces the town, while the Dublin Gate faces south-east towards Dublin. Originally, these gates would each have been fortified by a drawbridge and portcullis. Along the wall that fronts the river, the towers are rectangular, while the towers in the south wall are D-shaped.

The River Gate led to the Great Hall and to the Magdalen Tower. The Great Hall itself probably stood near the North Tower, but nothing remains of it today.

Excavations around the keep and the north-east wall produced a number of headless skeletons, which were no doubt the remains of executed prisoners. Finds here have also included pottery, arrowheads, an axe, silver coins and wine jugs.

---

 information

Contact details

Trim Castle
Trim
County Meath
Ireland

☎ +353 (0)46 943 8619

 Heritage Ireland site
www.heritageireland.ie
/en/midlandseastcoast
/trimcastle

Transport links

 From the M3, exit at
junction 5 and follow
signs for Trim

 Services run from Trim

ADARE CASTLE

SITE LOCATION: NEAR LIMERICK, IRELAND See map p.123 (21)
CONSTRUCTION DATE: 13TH CENTURY
SPECIAL FEATURES: MEDIEVAL BRIDGE

The impressive, though ruinous, Adare Castle in the west of Ireland still dominates the River Maigue, a tributary of the River Shannon, at what was once an important crossing point. Adare – from the Gaelic *Ath Dara*, meaning 'Ford of the Oak' – was built some time before 1227 and almost certainly replaced an earlier timber fortress.

Adare Castle is first mentioned in 1226. It was then owned by Geoffrey de Marisco, but as early as the mid-13th century it had passed into the hands of the FitzGeralds. Over the next 300 years, the castle was to change hands repeatedly after numerous bloody battles and insurrections – there were sieges in 1579, 1581 and 1600, each no doubt damaging the structure – until the Lord Protector of England, Scotland and Ireland, Oliver Cromwell ('that cursed devil', as he was known in Ireland), ordered the castle to be slighted, in other words rendered uninhabitable, in 1657.

Archaeological evidence suggests a construction date of about 1190, with the curtain walls being completed by 1240. The first castle consisted of a D-shaped moat or ditch with a square tower within and a great hall to the south. The tower had corner turrets projecting from the side walls and originally rose to three stories, with an entrance on the first floor. The great hall had magnificently decorated windows and at some later period a latrine was added.

By 1326, an aisled great hall had been added, with flanking kitchens and service rooms, in addition to the old hall. Repairs and new work continued until the 15th century, when the battlemented walls were built. A stone bridge spanning the River Maigue was built in medieval times, too.

The village that surrounds the castle – largely the work of the Quin family, Earls of Dunraven, who acquired the land after 1657 – dates mostly from the 19th century. It is one of the prettiest villages in Ireland, with thatched cottages and minimal amounts of modern building.

The present-day churches, Catholic and Protestant, incorporate the remains of the medieval Trinitarian, Franciscan and Augustinian abbeys that once stood here.

▲ *Adare Castle still dominates the River Maigue at what was once called* Ath Dara *('Ford of the Oak').*

ⓘ information

Contact details

Adare Heritage Centre
Main Street
Adare
County Limerick
Republic of Ireland

☎ +353 (0)61 396 666

🖳 **Adare Heritage Centre**

www.adareheritagecentre.ie

Transport links

🚗 Adare Castle is situated close to the main road-bridge over the River Maigue on the N21 approach from Limerick

TUDOR TO INDUSTRIAL PERIOD

AD 1485–1850

After the Dissolution of the Monasteries, brought about by Tudor king Henry VIII (r. 1509–47), the redistribution of wealth and resources in England helped lead to the rise of the mercantile classes and fuelled a new enthusiasm for secular building. Many of Britain's greatest houses were built during this period, their classically influenced designs inspired by the architecture and art of the Renaissance. With the coming of the Industrial Revolution, in the late 18th century, the country began to change as never before – factories with their own towns sprang up wherever fuel could be found to drive the new machinery. The history of our industrial heritage is a relatively new branch of archaeology, but it is just as fascinating as that of the Prehistoric, Roman or Medieval periods.

TUDOR TO INDUSTRIAL LOCATIONS

(1) Ye Olde Cheshire Cheese

(2) The George Inn

(3) Sutton House

(4) Bromham Mill

(5) Ironbridge

(6) Derwent Valley Mills

(7) Saltaire

(8) Dunseverick Castle

(9) Blaenavon

Shetland Islands

Inverness

Aberdeen

0 10 20 30 40 50 60 miles
0 10 20 40 60 80 100 km

EDINBURGH

Glasgow

Newcastle upon tyne

Londonderry

Donegal

NORTHERN
IRELAND   ⑧ BELFAST

York

⑦

Galway

DUBLIN

Liverpool   Manchester

IRELAND

Caernarfon

E N G L A N D

⑥

Norwich

Limerick

⑤ Birmingham

Cambridge

Killarney

Waterford

W A L E S

Oxford   ④

LONDON

⑨

CARDIFF

Bristol

Southampton

Dover

Brighton

Exeter

HAMPSTEAD   ③

L O N D O N

①

KENSINGTON   ②

GREENWICH

0   5 miles

0   5 km   DULWICH

YE OLDE CHESHIRE CHEESE

SITE LOCATION: FLEET STREET, LONDON   See map p.169 (1)

CONSTRUCTION DATE: 1667

SPECIAL FEATURES: UNALTERED INTERIORS

Fleet Street was always famously bordered by a mass of tangled courts and alleyways typical of a crowded city that had grown slowly over many centuries. Most of these courts and alleys are now built over or lined with dull office buildings but in Wine Office Court there is a most surprising survivor – a late 17th-century pub that looks exactly the same inside as it would have looked when it was first built.

What's more, the interior is not a recreation – the tables in the public bar, the fireplace, the décor and the pictures on the wall have all been here for at least 200 years. If we compare the interior of Ye Olde Cheshire Cheese to prints and drawings of early London coffee houses we realize that The Cheese is the last of these long-vanished features of London life.

The fame of the pub spread far and wide from the 1850s. The list of celebrities who drank here is extraordinary: writer Samuel Johnson is reported to have come here every night for years, along with his friend and biographer James Boswell; Charles Dickens spent many long evenings in the pub; and by the 20th century everyone from US president Theodore Roosevelt to writers Mark Twain and Arthur Conan Doyle dined and drank there.

◀ *The main bar of Ye Olde Cheshire Cheese has remained largely unaltered for more than two centuries.*

ⓘ information

Contact details

Ye Olde Cheshire Cheese
Wine Office Court
145 Fleet Street
London, EC4A 2BU

 +44 (0)20 7353 6170

 Traditional Pubs site
www.pubs.com/main_site
/pub_details.php?pub_id=154

Transport links

⊖ Blackfriars; Chancery Lane; Temple; Bank DLR

 City Thameslink; Blackfriars; Farringdon

THE GEORGE INN

SITE LOCATION: SOUTHWARK, LONDON

CONSTRUCTION DATE: LATE 17TH CENTURY

SPECIAL FEATURES: TAP ROOM AND TAVERN CLOCK

See map p.169

The George Inn is the last surviving galleried inn in London. This style of inn was common throughout the centuries when almost all transport was by horse.

In former times, there were at least half a dozen galleried inns in London. They were built around a courtyard and the rooms on each level gave way onto a walkway or gallery. It is a style of building that would have been familiar to Geoffrey Chaucer and William Shakespeare.

The inn would have been a hive of activity in its heyday. The courtyard enabled coaches to enter and be unloaded in the midst of the inn space. On the ground floor would have been public rooms for drinking and eating and above would have been the bedrooms. The George retains this arrangement.

▼ *The tap room of The George Inn looks today pretty much as it did in the 18th century.*

Although you can no longer stay at the inn, you may still drink in the bars below.

The oldest of The George's bars still has its 18th-century interiors – with tavern clock, crooked timber floors, two fireplaces and benches built into the walls. Sadly this small tap room, as it is known, though used until the 1980s, is no longer used as bar but it can still be visited. Only one side of what would have originally been a four-sided inn still exists but when you look up from the courtyard you can at least be sure that this is an authentic view into London's past. Charles Dickens even mentions The George by name in his novel *Little Dorrit* (1855–57).

There had been an inn on the site of The George since the 14th century but the present building dates from just after a huge fire that destroyed most of Southwark in 1676, after which it was rebuilt.

The arrival of the railways put paid to coaching inns but The George survived into

 Formerly known as The George and Dragon, the inn was named after St George.

the 20th century by using its yards as a hop market. It was gifted to the National Trust in 1937 after nearly being demolished.

(i) information

Contact details

The George Inn
77 Borough High Street
Southwark
London, SE1 1NH

☎ +44 (0)20 7407 2056

 National Trust site
www.nationaltrust.org.uk
/main/w-georgeinn

Transport links

⊖ London Bridge

🚆 London Bridge

SUTTON HOUSE

SITE LOCATION: HACKNEY, LONDON   See map p.169 ③
CONSTRUCTION DATE: *c*.1535
SPECIAL FEATURES: PANELLING AND FIREPLACES

Owned by the National Trust, Sutton House is a Tudor mansion left high and dry in one of the most run-down parts of London's Hackney. Despite its unpropitious location amid housing estates and dilapidated shopping precincts, Sutton House is a real gem. Many of the rooms still have their Tudor panelling, early wall paintings and original fireplaces. There are also artefacts and decorative schemes that reflect more recent owners.

Built in 1535 by Sir Ralph Sadleir, a courtier of Henry VIII (r. 1509–47), on the edge of what was then the tiny village of Hackney, Sutton House would have dazzled the locals when it was completed because it was built of brick, which was at that time hugely expensive.

After Sadleir's death, Sutton House passed through the hands of a series of wealthy merchants before becoming a girls' school in Victorian times. Gradually the city engulfed it, and although – remarkably – it was not significantly damaged, it declined badly and successive owners allowed it to decay. By the 1960s it was a hippy squat. Psychedelic murals painted in some of the rooms are still there, adding to the strange, multi-period feel of the house.

When Sutton House was built in 1535, Hackney was still a village some distance from London. ▶

ⓘ information

Contact details

Sutton House
2 and 4 Homerton High Street
Hackney, London, E9 6JQ

 +44 (0)20 8986 2264

 National Trust site
www.nationaltrust.org.uk
/main/w-suttonhouse

Transport links

 Hackney Central;
Hackney Downs

BROMHAM MILL

SITE LOCATION:	BROMHAM, BEDFORDSHIRE	See map p.169
CONSTRUCTION DATE:	LATE 17TH CENTURY	
SPECIAL FEATURES:	EEL TRAP AND IRON BREASTWHEEL	

Bromham Mill on the River Ouse in Bedfordshire has been grinding corn for centuries. Set in 2.8 hectares (7 acres) of water meadows and near the remarkable Georgian 26-arch Bromham Bridge, it is a glorious glimpse of Old England.

There has been a mill here since Saxon times, but the current picturesque building dates to the end of the 17th century, with Georgian and Victorian additions. It's a lovely mix of stonework, old brick and timber framing. Originally, there were two undershot wheels but an iron breastwheel installed in 1908 now provides the power for the wooden cogs and wheels.

The mill and the buildings that once surrounded it – blacksmith's shop, piggery and several cottages – were once a self-sufficient community. A great eel trap by the waterwheel is recorded as having taken more than 50 kilograms (110 pounds) of eels in one night and an apple orchard provided both food and just the right kind of timber for the gear teeth on the mill-wheels.

Bromham is important because it provides evidence of multi-use and reveals the central role that mills played in daily life in past centuries. They provided the flour to make bread – a staple food – as well as protein in the form of fish.

Bromham Mill is situated in almost 3 hectares (7 acres) of picturesque water meadows. ▶

---

information

Contact details

Bromham Mill
Bridge End, Bromham
Bedford, MK43 8LP

 +44 (0)1234 824330

 Brohman Hill
www.bedford.gov.uk/leisure_
and_culture/local_history_and
_heritage/bromham_mill.aspx

Transport links

 1.6 km (1 mile) from Bedford at the west end of Bromham Bridge, signposted from the A428

178

IRONBRIDGE

SITE LOCATION: NEAR TELFORD, SHROPSHIRE · See map p.169 **5**
CONSTRUCTION DATE: 1781
SPECIAL FEATURES: THE WORLD'S FIRST IRON BRIDGE

The small town of Ironbridge, designated a UNESCO World Heritage Site in 1986, is generally seen as the birthplace of the Industrial Revolution. Ironbridge's central claim within that context is the outstanding symbol of the new technology: the spectacular bridge of iron that spans the River Severn here.

The bridge – from which the town gets its name – is remarkable for a number of reasons, not least the fact that it is the world's first iron bridge. It was cast in sections in local foundries and built in 1781 by English ironmaster Abraham Darby III. Later industrial constructions and structures, including the roofs of

▼ *The techniques pioneered at Ironbridge were later used in the construction of many other buildings.*

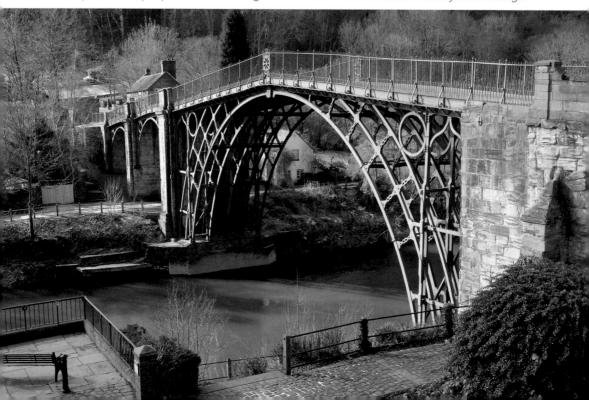

many famous railway stations, were based on the techniques pioneered here at Ironbridge. Apart from its industrial significance, much of the ironwork is decorative rather than structural.

The whole of this area of Shropshire, in the West Midlands, from Ironbridge itself up through the Ironbridge Gorge to Coalbrookdale, is a monument to the explosion of manufacturing that occurred in this part of the world in the late 18th century: nearby are the towns of Jackfield, Brosely and Coalport, which were all once famous for the manufacture of ceramic and iron goods.

The former importance of the area can be judged by the fact that there are no fewer than ten museums devoted to the early industrial period. In addition, there are restored workers' cottages and factory owners' houses, canals and warehouses, all once parts of a scene of frenzied and constant activity.

 Much of the bridge's ironwork is decorative rather than structural.

Today, of course, these places look clean, tidy and well-groomed; but about 150 years ago, they were blackened with the smoke and dirt from the fires in warrens of kilns, foundries and quarries – and the 'dark satanic mills' of which William Blake wrote in his poem 'And Did Those Feet in Ancient Time' (*c.*1808).

ⓘ information

Contact details

Ironbridge
Shropshire

☎ +44 (0)1952 433424

 Ironbridge Museums
www.ironbridge.org.uk

Transport links

🚗 Exit at junctions 4 or 6 of the M54 and follow signs to Ironbridge Gorge

DERWENT VALLEY MILLS

SITE LOCATION: DERWENT VALLEY, DERBYSHIRE   See map p.169
CONSTRUCTION DATE: FROM 1771
SPECIAL FEATURES: MACHINERY FROM THE EARLY
                  INDUSTRIAL REVOLUTION

Derwent Valley Mills in Derbyshire is one of the great British centres of industrial archaeology. It was here in 1771 that water power was first used to mass-produce textiles, a movement that spurred the nascent Industrial Revolution.

The Derwent Valley had the advantages of a powerful river and – rather sadly from our 21st-century viewpoint – abundant local child labour.

Interestingly, the famous spinning jenny was not suitable for these early factories since it was too complex to be operated by children. Pioneers such as Sir Richard Arkwright invented other machines – most notably the Arkwright frame – that could be operated by children and that carried out many, though by no means all, of the processes involved in producing yarn.

Today, the Derwent Valley World Heritage Site includes not just the factories and machines that began the industrial revolution, but also examples of workers' cottages. Visitors can see how the factory owners also owned and ran shops and other services – as well, of course, as the workers' homes. In effect, the factory workers' whole lives were controlled by the mill owners.

◀ *The River Derwent was used to power the mass production of textiles at the mills.*

ⓘ information

Contact details

Derwent Valley Mills
PO Box 6297
Matlock, Derbyshire
DE4 3WJ

 +44 (0)1629 539781

 Derwent Valley Mills
www.derwentvalleymills.org

Transport links

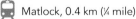 Matlock, 0.4 km (¼ mile)

182

SALTAIRE

SITE LOCATION: NEAR BRADFORD, WEST YORKSHIRE   See map p.169 (7)

CONSTRUCTION DATE: EARLY 19TH CENTURY

SPECIAL FEATURES: WORKERS' COTTAGES

Just to the north of Bradford and deep in Yorkshire's Brontë Country is the village of Saltaire. What makes this place so special is that it was built as a 'model' or ideal village by the great mill owner Sir Titus Salt, one of the most remarkable industrialists of that great period of industrial expansion that made Britain the commercial centre of the world. Salt was determined to provide decent accommodation for the workers at his textile mill on the River Aire, during a time when most factory owners allowed their workers to live in conditions of the utmost poverty and degradation.

Saltaire is such a remarkable place that it was designated a UNESCO World Heritage Site in 2001. The houses and shops are simple, brick-built and by no means grand, but compared to the Victorian slums of Manchester and Leeds, Saltaire must have seemed like heaven to 19th-century industrial workers. The streets let in the light; the houses have moderately sized windows and are solid and well made.

Unlike those pious mill and factory owners who went devoutly to church each Sunday but were happy at the same time to work their staff – many of whom would have been children – to death, Sir Titus Salt was both a businessman and a genuine, practical philanthropist and Saltaire is his monument.

Developed during the Industrial Revolution, Saltaire is better known today as a place ▶
where workers were treated remarkably benevolently by the standards of the time.

 ## information

Contact details

Saltaire Village
Near Bradford
West Yorkshire

 **Saltaire Village**
www.saltairevillage.info

Transport links

 Saltaire

DUNSEVERICK CASTLE

184

SITE LOCATION: COUNTY ANTRIM, IRELAND   See map p.169 (8)

CONSTRUCTION DATE: *c.*16TH CENTURY

SPECIAL FEATURES: ON DIRECT ROUTE TO TARA, POWER BASE
                                      OF THE HIGH KINGS OF IRELAND

All that remains of the grand castle that once stood at one of Ireland's most historic sites is a ruined tower – for Dunseverick Castle was destroyed in 1642 by a Scottish army sent to put down a rebellion by three Irish aristocrats: Rory O'More, Sir Pheilim O'Neill and Lord Maquire. General Robert Munro was given the task

▼ *Although little remains of Dunseverick Castle today, it is one of Ireland's most historically important sites.*

of crushing the insurrection and destroying the rebels' stronghold.

The ruins that can be seen today date back to the mid-16th century, when the castle was built by the MacDonnell family. The site had always been a strategically important one, surrounded by the sea on three sides and on a direct route to Tara, the power base of the High Kings, who ruled Ireland until end of the 12th century.

The first fortress was built here in about 1500BC by the Celtic king Sobairce, who ruled the ancient kingdom of Dalriada. This realm stretched from the north Antrim coast to Scotland's Mull of Kintyre; the modern name 'Dunseverick' derives from *Dunsobairce*, meaning 'Fortress of Sobairce'.

Many of the great heroes of Irish storytelling were said to have come to this remote and atmospheric spot – including, to name but two, Turlough and Cuchulain.

St Patrick – the patron saint of Ireland – is also said to have visited Dunseverick. *Tubber Phadrick*, a well near the cliff edge, is named after him. Legend has it that Patrick baptized a local man called Olcan who later became bishop of all Ireland, dying about AD480. Towards the end of the first millennium AD, Dunseverick Castle – among many settlements on the Irish coast – was targeted by Viking raiders.

It is important to remember that, despite their often remote locations, castles such as Dunseverick were part of an interlinked system of fortresses that were strewn across the country. All the kings who lived here were in touch continually with the wider world.

The castle and the peninsula on which it stands were given to the National Trust in 1962 by local farmer Jack McCurdy. In 1978, part of the ruins fell into the sea.

 # information

Contact details

Dunseverick
County Antrim
Northern Ireland

 Dunseverick Castle
www.thenorthernireland guide.co.uk/blog /dunseverick-castle

Transport links

 Dunseverick Castle is about 15 km (9½ miles) from Ballycastle on the A2 towards the Giant's Causeway

BLAENAVON

SITE LOCATION: NEAR ABERGAVENNY, WALES   See map p.169 (9)
CONSTRUCTION DATE: LATE 18TH CENTURY
SPECIAL FEATURES: COTTAGES, STEAM TRAINS AND EARLY FACTORIES

The works at Blaenavon in South Wales were abandoned almost overnight, and as a result they have survived virtually intact into an age when we value them for what they tell us about the early industrial era.

Blaenavon was once one of the great mining and industrial centres of the world. It achieved its industrial fame because it was superbly located for the raw materials necessary for early manufacturing processes – ironstone, limestone and timber.

Manufacturing at Blaenavon actually goes back much further than the Industrial Revolution: minerals and timber were being worked here from the 16th century, if not earlier. The town itself, however, was founded as late as 1787 when Thomas Hill, Thomas Hopkins and Benjamin Pratt leased 18 square kilometres (7 square miles) of moorland from Lord Abervagenny. They built Wales's first real industrial plant, with three furnaces powered by steam rather than the water-powered furnaces that had previously been the norm.

By 1789, iron began to pour out of Blaenavon along with coal, both of which disappeared into Midland factories, whose appetite for them seemed insatiable. These materials were also sent abroad via the Brecknock and Abergavenny Canal.

A decade after that first plant at Blaenavon was opened, it was the biggest industrial plant in Wales. Workers flooded in, and many of the cottages that were built for them still survive as a fascinating reminder of domestic life at the beginning of the Industrial Revolution. The invention and arrival of the steam train helped Blaenavon grow even faster.

The fall of Blaenavon began in 1876 when two cousins, Percy Carlisle Gilchrist and Sidney Gilchrist Thomas, working at the plant, invented an improved process for converting pig iron into steel. This breakthrough meant that many other plants in the world could now make their own high-quality steel. By the beginning of the 20th century, Germany and the United States no longer needed Blaenavon steel. The last Blaenavon furnace shut down in 1904, although coal continued to be mined until 1980, when the last mine closed.

 The abandoned industrial plant of Blaenavon in Wales became a World Heritage Site in 2000.

The industrial archaeology of Blaenavon is fascinating and uniquely valuable. The Big Pit and the Old Ironworks can still be seen alongside old tramways and railway tracks, quarries, reservoirs, disused mines, kilns and chimneys – and the Hills Tramway, a remarkable trolley-rail system that carried coal from Blaenavon to Garndyrys.

(i) information

Contact details

Blaenavon World Heritage Centre
Church Road
NP4 9AS

☎ +44 (0)1495 742333

www **Blaenavon World Heritage site**
www.world-heritage-blaenavon.org.uk/en/homepage.aspx

Transport links

 From the M4, follow the brown tourism signs from junction 25A or J26. Also signposted off the A465 at Brynmawr and Abergavenny

 Service X30 from Newport

INDEX

ACKNOWLEDGEMENTS

Thanks to all those who put up with my persistent and endless queries and to James, Alex, Katy, Nutmeg and Wadster. Thanks also to Charlotte Macey and Jolyon Goddard who did all the hard work.